Everywoman's Canning Book

The A B C of Safe Home Canning and Preserving

by

Mrs. Mary Catherine Burke Hughes

APPLEWOOD BOOKS
Bedford, Massachusetts

Everywoman's Canning Book

was originally published in

1918

ISBN: 978-1-4290-1056-6

Thank you for purchasing an Applewood book.
Applewood reprints America's lively classics—
books from the past that are still of interest
to the modern reader.
For a free copy of
a catalog of our
bestselling
books,
write
to us at:
Applewood Books
Box 365
Bedford, MA 01730
or visit us on the web at:
For cookbooks: foodsville.com
For our complete catalog: awb.com

Prepared for publishing by HP

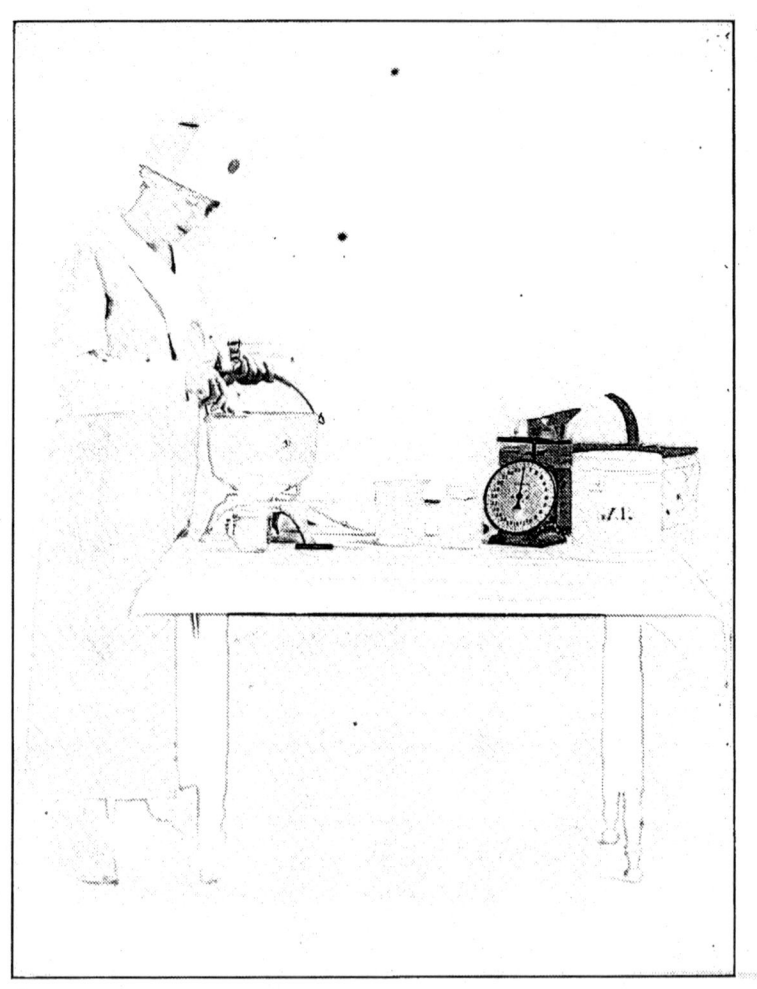

EVERYWOMAN'S CANNING BOOK

The A B C of Safe Home Canning and Preserving by the Cold Pack Method

MARY B. HUGHES

This book has been examined before publication and is found to conform to the principles of the United States Food Administration in regard to the conservation of foods.

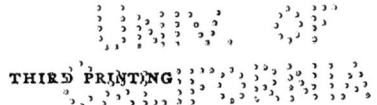

THIRD PRINTING

1918

WHITCOMB & BARROWS :: PUBLISHERS
BOSTON :: :: :: MASSACHUSETTS

TX603
H7

Copyright 1918
By Whitcomb & Barrows

DEDICATED

TO ALL THE VOLUNTEERS

who worked through the hot summer days, during the season of 1917, in the Food Conservation Drive for War Relief at Mrs. Hemenway's Canning Kitchen, Boston.

Special thanks are due

MRS. AUGUSTUS HEMENWAY

whose enthusiasm and leadership inspired hundreds of women to gather at her home, in patriotic service, to can and dry the garden surplus sent from the surrounding countryside.

M. B. H.

415286

CONTENTS

	PAGE
FOREWORD	vii
GENERAL DIRECTIONS FOR HOME CANNING	1
EQUIPMENT	7
QUESTIONS MOST FREQUENTLY ASKED	10
PREPARATION OF HOME-CANNED PRODUCTS FOR THE TABLE	15
CANNING OF VEGETABLES	17
SOUP MIXTURES	27
CANNING MEAT AND FISH	30
CANNING FRUITS	32
COLD WATER METHOD FOR PRESERVING FRUIT	40
JELLY MAKING	41
FRUIT JUICES	51
PICKLING	56
MISCELLANEOUS CONTRIBUTED RECIPES	72
DRY YOUR VEGETABLES AND FRUITS	85

FOREWORD

"Gather up the fragments that remain; that nothing be lost."

ECONOMIC conditions make it imperative that we as a nation produce and conserve more food. Every housekeeper should prepare for the reconstruction period that will follow the war, when, owing to the demands to be made upon our markets by the whole world, and to the fact that the man power of civilization will be short and crippled, food will be less abundant and much higher in price than it is now.

Comparatively few housewives, up to the present time, have gone into the fields to help in the production and harvesting of food supplies, yet the day is not distant when the American housewife will manage a hoe quite as easily as she handles her broom and duster now. By thus entering the ranks of producers, she will gain in health and happiness as well as materially.

The most practical way to conserve foods is to can or dry them for future use when the harvests are abundant and foodstuffs are low in price. To encourage housewives to do more canning, preserving, and drying, I have prepared this book, dealing with the problems of home canning as they developed at Mrs. Hemenway's Canning Kitchen for War Relief, in Boston. The conditions there, under which 8,000 jars were safely sealed for winter use, without loss, were the same as those found in the average household. Five years' experience canning my own garden surplus taught me many practical points which have been incorporated here, with the hope of aiding other housekeepers in their canning.

FOREWORD

Owing to scientific methods, canning need no longer be the hot, arduous task that it was even five years ago. For the simplified, shortened method of canning called "Cold-Pack," the housewives of America owe thanks to the United States Department of Agriculture.

Lack of sugar need not affect the amount of canning done during the war period, for experiments have proved that fruits keep just as well without sugar if they are properly sealed. Sugar can be added when the fruits are served.

Acknowledgments are due Mrs. Everell F. Sweet, South Natick; Miss Louisa Sohier, Wellesley Hills; Miss Marion Bryant, Newtonville; and to many others, who have contributed choice old family recipes to make this book of value.

Two recipes, "Dixie Relish" and "Cranberry Catsup," are taken from Miss Ola Powell's book, "Successful Canning and Preserving," published by J. B. Lippincott Company, and used with the gracious consent of the author and publisher.

Special attention is called to the paragraphs on Correct Processing and Preparation of Home-Canned Products for the Table, pp. 4 and 15.

M. B. H.

WELLESLEY, February, 1918.

CALIFORNIA

GENERAL DIRECTIONS FOR HOME CANNING

CANNING of fruits and vegetables by the process known as Cold-Pack[1] may, for convenience, be divided into six steps: Preparation of Materials, Blanching, Plunging, Packing, Processing, and Sealing. Each step is important, and a clear understanding of these terms and familiarity with each process are necessary to success, since they are used throughout the book.

Preparation. No vegetables or fruits which are withered or unsound should be used. If possible, pick materials the morning of the day they are to be canned. Vegetables and fruits lose much of their flavor by standing, and the fresher they are the better will be the results obtained. Grade, especially for ripeness and size, and pick over carefully. Do not can fruit until it is ripe, unless a recipe calls specifically for green fruit. Have plenty of fresh, clean water, to wash grit and dirt from vegetables.

Blanching. Parboiling is another term for this process commonly used by the housewife. Blanching is necessary to shrink the product, to start the flow of coloring matter, and to eliminate objectionable acids.

Put vegetables (and some fruits) in a cheesecloth sack or wire basket, and plunge into enough fresh boiling water to immerse completely the material to be blanched.

---

[1] Cold-Pack Canning was introduced by the Department of Agriculture in 1915, and is the simplest, most up-to-date method of canning fruits and vegetables. It is indorsed throughout the country by canning experts and practical housekeepers who are familiar with it.

The time for blanching varies with different vegetables and fruits, and vegetables require longer blanching than fruits. It is important to count the time of blanching from the minute the water begins to boil after the product is immersed.

Blanch greens and green vegetables (like spinach, Swiss chard, asparagus, etc.) over live steam, as the volatile oils are lost when blanched in water, and special food value is wasted. A convenient way to blanch over steam is as follows: Take one and a half yards of cheesecloth; make a hammock over a wash boiler with a little boiling water in it. Tie the two ends of the cheesecloth in the handles at the sides of the boiler, put the greens in the suspended cheesecloth, put on the cover of the boiler, and steam the required time.

In canning berries and all soft fruits, blanching is dispensed with.

Plunging. Have at hand a large bowl of fresh, cold water, preferably with ice in it (ice is not a necessity), and plunge the vegetables or fruits directly from the boiling water into the cold water. Take out immediately. The plunge should not require more than ten seconds. Never plunge more than one set of vegetables or fruits in the same water. In plunging all vegetables, but especially spinach and other greens, care must be taken that the cold plunge affects the inner portion of the product as well as the surface. Plunging is necessary to loosen the skins, to harden the pulp, to set the coloring matter, and to facilitate the packing.

Packing. The material is now ready to go into freshly washed jars. For vegetables, add hot water, and salt for seasoning—a teaspoonful to a quart. For fruits, hot syrup or hot water is used. Fill the jar to one-half inch of the top, put on a new rubber which has been scalded, adjust the cover, and put one clamp of the bail in place. If the jar has a screw top, put the cap in position and screw lightly, using thumb and little finger for pressure.

Processing. This part of the work is of the greatest importance. After each jar is partially sealed as above, place on a wire rack in the bottom of a wash boiler. Fill the boiler with water until it reaches two or three inches over the top of the jars. Have the water in the boiler about the same temperature as that of the liquid poured over the material in the jars. This will keep the jars from cracking. Put the cover on the boiler and bring the water to a quick boil. Count the time for processing from the minute you hear the water boiling and bubbling actively in the container. Do not let the fire get low and the water stop boiling, for good material is ruined by careless processing.

Sealing. Immediately after the termination of the processing period, remove the jars from the boiler. A buttonhook makes a very good aid if the jar has a bail. For screw-top jars it is necessary to buy a commercial jar holder. These can be bought for a small sum. Place the hot jars on a table out of a draft, put down second clamp of bail or tighten screw-top cap with full strength, and invert to cool. Watch closely for leaks. If leakage occurs, tighten the bail. It is well to cover the jars, while cooling, with a clean cloth or towel. If a large number of jars are processed at once, do not place them closely together to cool, but separate them on different tables, so they will cool rapidly. Slow cooling of the jars is undesirable, and affects the flavor of the product.

Testing the Seal. After processing, set the jars aside for a few days before putting away in the preserve closet. To see if the seal is perfect, unfasten both clamps of the bail and lift the jar by the top. If the top comes off easily, the seal is imperfect. Either reprocess the full length of time given in the tables, or, if fermentation has started, throw material away.

Correct Processing is absolutely essential to successful canning, and to understand the importance of it, let us consider why we process. Every piece of fruit or vegetable, no matter how fresh, will have on its surface tiny, invisible microörganisms. The air contains many microörganisms, an important thing to remember in canning. If living organisms remain in the jars, they increase rapidly, causing food to decay and spoil. We "process" to kill the microörganisms, and thus to render food in the jars sterile; and we "seal" to keep out other organisms which are in the air.

Microörganisms are divided into three main groups: yeasts, bacteria, and molds. In canning, we may find yeast plants on fruits and vegetables, bacteria on vegetables and meats, and molds from the air may form on jams and jellies. Canning immediately after the vegetables are gathered, and cleanliness in all handling, lessens the danger from these organisms.

Different organisms require different degrees of heat and different lengths of time to render them sterile or inactive. Yeasts are killed by lower degrees of heat than bacteria. A short period of processing, from fifteen to twenty-five minutes, with the water actively boiling around the jars, is all that is necessary for the heat to penetrate sufficiently to kill the yeasts on fruit; while bacteria in the spore state may resist two and three hours' active boiling. Spores have been known to resist twelve hours' processing in the hot water bath, at a temperature of 212° F., and to become active in the jars after ten or twelve hours. This is the reason that an occasional jar of beans or corn may spoil, while others done in the same way at the same time keep in perfect condition.

There is only one short process by which the spores in vegetables may be killed, and that is by the use of the Steam Pressure Canner, with which a temperature of 250° F. can be obtained. These pressure canners are expensive, but they can be used for a great deal of cooking in addition to the canning, hence are desirable when they can be afforded.

The Intermittent or Fractional Method of Canning. This great resistant power of spores in vegetables makes the Intermittent or Fractional Method of canning the method chosen by some experts, especially for peas, corn, Lima beans, and string beans, on which bacteria are most likely to be found. Some practical housekeepers, who have been most successful in their home canning, are inclined to look with disfavor on the intermittent process, because of the additional labor involved in processing the jars three successive days. This method, they feel, discourages rather than encourages much canning. It is, however, widely used in the South, and it is well for every woman interested in canning her garden surplus to know how to do the intermittent method, since some years the bacteria are particularly virulent, and spoilage after careful processing would indicate that the intermittent sterilization would be best for that particular kind of vegetable.

The principle of the intermittent method of sterilization is that spores not killed after the first processing will be less resistant and will probably be killed after the second day's processing, and that after the third day's processing there is very little chance of their living to do harm to the product.

To process intermittently, partially seal the product in the usual way and process one hour. Remove jar from container, seal, and set aside for twenty-four hours. On the second day, lift the spring of the clamp and set the partially sealed jar back in the processing bath, and process again for one hour. Remove, seal, and set aside for another twenty-four hours. On the third day, repeat this process. The jar is then ready to seal and put away.

Fruits are never subjected to the intermittent method.

It is *absolutely necessary* to follow accurately the time given in the tables for processing, if success is to be assured. It is quite common to hear the amateur say, in reporting failures, that she processed the beans thirty minutes, just as long as she ever cooks them for the table, and they spoiled. Thirty minutes will cook tender beans and make them edible, but it takes three hours' continuous cooking to kill the spores living in them, and to prepare them so they will keep all winter. Do not compare the time you would cook your product for the table with the length of time it needs processing. *Follow your time table if you wish for success.*

Once sterilized, if for any reason the jar must be opened, even though the cover is lifted only for a second, be sure and place again in the sterilizing bath and process for ten minutes, otherwise organisms enter with the air, multiply rapidly, and spoilage results.

EQUIPMENT

IT is claimed that eighty-five per cent of all human ailments are caused by improper diet. Four months of the year, when there is an abundance of fresh fruits and vegetables, we eat plenty of them; the remainder of the year our diet is highly concentrated, with an excess of protein foods. The fiber, mineral salts, and acids found in fruits and vegetables are a daily requirement of the body if health is to be maintained. Home canning should be so planned that the family will have a jar of fruit and a jar of vegetables every day when fresh supplies cannot be obtained. In the beginning of the season, if the housewife will purchase two jars for each day of the winter months (pints or quarts, according to the size of the family), she will then have her goal set ahead of her, and will take delight in reaching it by the end of the season.

Jars. "What kind of jar is best?" is frequently asked. This is a matter of individual preference. Jars with wide necks and straight sides are easily packed and cleaned. Whether the glass is green or white makes no difference in the keeping of the product. The green glass does not prevent bleaching when the products are exposed to light. Fruits and vegetables have a much finer appearance when packed in a good, clear, colorless glass.

Do not buy cheap jars, as invariably they are defective or of poor glass, and crack easily. A cheap jar is most expensive in the end. Every jar, before being packed, should be examined carefully for defects. Run the finger around the edge to see if the glass is chipped; also fill the jar with water and watch for tiny air holes. Air bubbles will be seen to rise from the side of the jar when there is a defect in the glass. Discard every defective jar.

If screw-top jars are used, care must be taken to see that the cap is not bent and that the rim is perfect. Adjust the rubber and screw on the cap tightly. Invert. If there is leakage, try a cap which has never been used. When a bail is used, test it with the rubber and top adjusted, to see if it works properly, before filling the jar.

Rubber Rings. The quality of rubber ring used is of the greatest importance. A jar cannot be air-tight, or remain so for any length of time, unless the rubber ring is of the proper texture. After the contents are processed, the possibility of keeping the jar air-tight depends on the rubber used. A good ring must be both wide and thick, and of such rubber that it can be stretched ten inches or more, when it will snap back into shape and not break or crack. *It is never safe to use the same rubber more than once.* Use the rings which come with the jars only for pickles and preserves, which keep without an air-tight seal. Never buy cheap rubbers.

Sterilizers. For those who wish to do canning for commercial purposes, steam pressure outfits are to be recommended. They save time, labor, and fuel, and give excellent results. They are, however, by no means essential to success, and the wash boiler is all that is necessary for family use. When only a few jars are to be processed at a time, it is more economical to use a smaller container, thereby eliminating the heating of unnecessary water. A lard pail or a new garbage can, or a stew kettle with a tight cover and a false bottom, makes a good sterilizer.

Utensils, etc. Other items of equipment are cheesecloth, plenty of clean towels, several large bowls, paring knives, teaspoon, wooden spoon, colander and pestle, cake racks, scales, and timepiece. Plenty of fresh, clean water is essential.

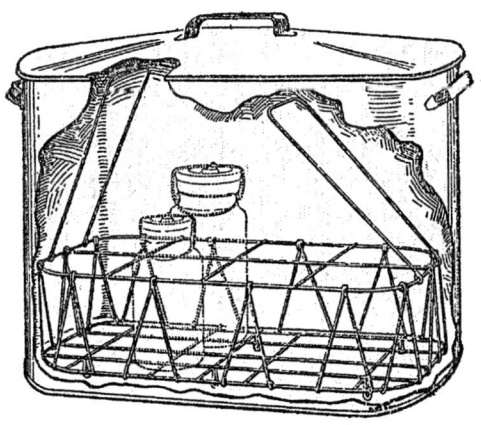

QUESTIONS MOST FREQUENTLY ASKED

Should the jars be boiled before using?

This one problem seems to give more anxiety than any other to the beginner in canning. It is *not necessary* to boil either jars or rubbers before using them. Wash thoroughly and rinse in hot water. They are sterilized at the same time the contents of the jars are processed or sterilized. Any previous boiling is superfluous. Much unnecessary drudgery is eliminated when housekeepers fully appreciate the fact that in cold-pack canning it is not necessary to handle the jars out of boiling water. To have them clean is enough.

Should the jars touch each other in the processing?

It does no harm if the jars touch each other or the side of the container in the processing. Arranging hay, cardboard, or wrapping the jars in cloth to keep them from touching, is unnecessary labor.

It is unwise to place the jars on top of each other in processing, for the air in the lower jars cannot expand. This will crack the jars. If a second tier is needed, have a rack fitted in the boiler, which will act as a second shelf.

What must be done when the rubbers bulge?

If a rubber bulges when it is taken from the boiler, press it back immediately with the finger, set the jar in the sterilizing bath, and leave for ten minutes.

Is it necessary to have the water come over the top of the jars?

It is important to have the water come over the top of the jars to a depth of two inches or more. In processing vegetables which require a long period of sterilizing, such as corn, beans, and peas, have the water three or four inches over the top of the jars. If the boiler is not air-tight, the escaping steam will greatly reduce the water around the jars. Plenty of water in the boiler to start with eliminates the possibility of having the boiler get dry.

Do bubbles indicate spoilage?

By no means. Bubbles usually take care of themselves in a few days. If there is any uncertainty about the jar, set it one side for a few days; and if the bubbles are still present, reprocess for one-half the original period. If a frothy white collection of bubbles appears at the top, usually the jar is defective. In this case use the product at once on the table, or put into a new jar and resterilize for one-half the original period.

Why do the jars break in the sterilizing bath?

When jars break in the sterilizing bath, first see if the second clamp was put down by mistake, or if the rack was forgotten in the boiler. If the jars are set in water of a higher temperature than the liquid in the jar, they will crack. *Some breakage is due to defective glass.* When the bottom of the jar drops out and leaves a clean, straight cut around the jar, the fault is with the glass. If jars are carefully handled, the percentage of breakage is very small.

Should the product shrink?

Some shrinkage is expected, but when the product shrinks to any great extent, it means careless blanching and a poor pack. Jars do not have to be full to keep. Therefore it is unnecessary to open the jar and fill it up with boiling water. If the jar is opened (which is inadvisable) and boiling water or hot syrup added, it must be processed for one-half the original time. By opening the jar and adding water, the housekeeper does not in any way add to the food value of the jar, and gives herself a great deal of unnecessary work.

What is meant by flat-sour?

Flat-sour is a term used to denote spoilage that is not detected until the jar is opened. A product which has flat-soured, however slightly, should never be eaten. Just what specific bacteria cause flat-sour is not known, but it is quite safe to say that home canners whose methods are clean and who use fresh products, and *process the required time according to the time tables,* are never troubled with flat-sour.

What causes beets to darken?

Beets will turn dark if exposed to a strong light, and also if they are allowed to stand in the jars without water for any length of time before they are processed. Jars should be filled and processed immediately.

What is a good storage place?

A cool, dark place is the best for storing home-canned products. A cellar preserve closet is not a necessity. A pantry near the kitchen, where the jars will be convenient when wanted, makes as good a storage place as any. The jars should be protected from the light.

If the jars are placed in the cellar, they must be looked at occasionally, as the molds which attack rubbers in a damp atmosphere cause them to decay, letting the air into the jars and causing spoilage.

What are preserving powders?

Preserving powders are good things to let alone. Housewives are cautioned against buying these so-called preserving powders from agents who go from door to door. Benzoic acid, salicylic acid, boric acid, and formaldehyde are sometimes sold to shorten the time of processing fruits and vegetables.

Under no circumstances should the housewife use any preservative in her canning. Process the full time given in the time tables and preservatives will be unnecessary. Their use is not only very dangerous, but also expensive.

What would you most caution the beginner against?

Against following everybody's advice as to canning. Do not look for short cuts. There are none. Follow a reliable guide and remember that in canning there is one best method, which will insure uniform success year after year.

Are jars superior to cans for home canning?

It is generally agreed that fruits and vegetables which are canned in glass are of a finer flavor than those canned in tins, though their nutritive value is no higher. Experts tell us there is nothing about the use of a good tin can which is harmful. For home canning, however, glass jars are to be recommended, as they last from year to year.

When several bushels of tomatoes or peaches are to be canned, to take care of a large surplus, the cost of the container is an important consideration. Cans are much cheaper than jars. A special outfit must be purchased if tin is to be used.

What does it cost to can fruits and vegetables?

Prices vary so that it is impossible to give a definite answer to this question. The first-year cost is the greatest, since it includes equipment and jars. A conservative estimate shows a saving of seventy per cent on all home-canned products over the market price for the same varieties canned in tin.

PREPARATION OF HOME-CANNED PRODUCTS FOR THE TABLE

ALL canned vegetables should be heated through to the boiling point before being served. In home canning, where preservatives should never be used, this is a matter of wise precaution, that any bacteria which may have developed may be destroyed. Scientists who have made special investigations of home-canned products inform us that there is not the slightest danger of "botulism," a rare form of poisoning from eating home-canned goods, if the product is first boiled for a few minutes after being taken from the jar. This does not mean that products must be eaten while hot. In the case of canned vegetables to be used in salads, they may be boiled and set aside until chilled through.

The flavor of all canned products is greatly improved when the jar is opened six hours before serving. Pour the contents of the jar into a large bowl and set aside in the icebox. Oxygen will then have permeated the product before it is served. Vegetables requiring a long processing period, like corn, beans, greens, etc., are especially improved in flavor if allowed to stand out of the jar for six hours before being used.

How to Open a Jar

Jars are sometimes hard to open. This way is recommended: Using a thin knife blade, such as a paring knife or pen knife, insert the point under the lower edge of the rubber and press firmly. This will usually let in enough air to release the air pressure on the top of the jar. After several attempts, if this is not successful, place the jar in cold water in a deep dish. Have the water come over the top. Bring to the boiling point for a few minutes. The jar will then open easily.

CANNING OF VEGETABLES

IN order to use these recipes successfully, there must be familiarity with all the details of the General Directions, pp. 1–6.

Asparagus

Blanch 8 minutes   Plunge until chilled to touch
Process 2½ hours

Only tender, fresh asparagus should be used, and stalks should be of good thickness. Wash, cut to proper lengths to fit jars, and remove scales with sharp knife. Lay in small piles, heads together, in a square of cheesecloth, and tie ends. Blanch in boiling water to cover for eight minutes. Plunge; pack in jars with heads up. Add a teaspoon of salt for each quart; fill jars with hot water within one-half inch of top. Place rubber and cap in position, partially seal, and process two and one-half hours. Asparagus must not be too closely packed, or the stalks will be broken in getting it out from the jars. Wrap jars in paper to prevent bleaching.

String Beans

Blanch   Plunge   Process 3 hours
Omit   Omit

Green string beans or butter beans are perhaps the easiest of all vegetables to can. Unlike corn, they are much better canned than dried. It has been the experience of many who have canned beans for years that no special advantage comes from blanching or plunging them. Omitting the blanching saves much labor. Have the beans as fresh from the vines as possible, and be sure all pods are tender. Wash, string, cut in convenient lengths, or leave them whole if desired. Pack in freshly washed jars within one inch of the top, cover with boiling water, add one teaspoonful of salt for each quart; adjust rubber, cap, and clamp lightly. Process for three hours. Uniform results are not obtained if less than three hours is given. Blanching does not affect the time of processing.

For those who wish to blanch beans and experiment to see if it improves the flavor of the product, the following table is given: Blanch 5 minutes. Plunge. Process 3 hours.

Lima Beans or Shell Beans

| Blanch | Plunge | Process 3 hours |
| Omit | Omit | |

Pick before pods become dry and cracked. Can as soon as possible. Shell; pack lightly in jars to within one inch of top. Do not press down. Add salt, a teaspoon to a quart, and hot water to fill crevices. Adjust rubber, cover, and seal lightly. Process three hours.

Boston Baked Beans

To serve home-baked Boston beans the year round, without the inconvenience of a hot kitchen fire in the summer, or to have them as an emergency dish for lunch, plan as follows: When baking beans in the customary way, cook an extra pint of dry beans. When cooked, have at hand two hot pint jars with rubbers in place. Fill with beans within one inch of top, put on cover, and seal lightly. Process one and one-half hours. Beans prepared thus will keep indefinitely, and no commercial brand of baked beans on the market compares with home-baked beans canned in this way.

Beets or Carrots

Blanch 15 minutes   Plunge until chilled
Process 2½ hours

Beets and carrots are winter as well as summer vegetables. While they can be bought in the market all winter and keep well in a root cellar, nevertheless it is very practical for the housewife to have a supply of them in her preserve closet, ready for immediate use. The longer beets and carrots are out of the ground, the longer cooking they require, and they lose much of their fine flavor and become woody. When canned directly out of the ground, they are sweet and most palatable; and the housewife who makes vegetable or meat hash frequently, appreciates having on hand canned beets and carrots.

In selecting beets or carrots to can whole, the smaller ones, which run twenty-five to a quart, make the choicest looking pack. When the farmer is thinning out his rows, gather those that are cast aside, and use the best for canning.

Scrub vegetables with a brush. Blanch fifteen minutes, plunge in cold water, and leave until cool enough to handle. Scrape with a dull knife; pack in jars, whole or sliced; add salt, a teaspoon to a quart; fill jars with hot water within one-half inch of top, adjust rubber and cap, clamp lightly, and process two and one-half hours.

In blanching beets, leave two or three inches of the stem and all of the root on, to keep them from bleeding. Well-prepared beets look pale when first taken from the processing bath, but soon regain their color. When cool, wrap the jars in paper to prevent bleaching, or set away in a dark closet.

Cauliflower

Blanch 5 minutes   Plunge 10 seconds   Process $1\frac{1}{2}$ hours

Break cauliflower into flowerets. Put into cold brine (one-half cup salt to one gallon of water) and let stand for one and one-half hours. Blanch in boiling water five minutes and plunge in cold water. Pack in hot jars, fill with boiling water within one-half inch of top, add teaspoon of salt for each quart, adjust rubber and cap, seal lightly, and process one and one-half hours.

To Serve. Heat to boiling point, pour off water, and add white sauce, butter or butter substitute, and seasoning.

Corn

Blanch 5 minutes   Plunge 10 seconds   Process 4 hours

Various experiments have proved that to the taste of many persons corn is more palatable dried than canned. (See last chapter.) Many housekeepers, however, have canned their surplus corn for years with satisfactory results. Great care must be used and instructions followed. Government experts teach that once the corn is pulled from the stalk, the amount of its sugar diminishes rapidly and changes into starch. Over night the ear loses fifty per cent of its sugar, so to get the best results it is necessary to can the product, if possible, within an hour from the time it is brought from the fields. Select the corn between the milk and the dough stage. At this stage, it is not too ripe, neither is it undeveloped. A little experience is necessary to judge accurately the best time for canning. Never can corn that has been packed in bulk in baskets, and has become heated through.

Remove husks and silk. Blanch on the cob for five minutes. Plunge into cold water, then cut from the cob, being careful not to cut into the cob. Pack directly into jars, within one inch of the top. Add one teaspoon of sugar and one of salt for a quart, adjust rubber, cover, and clamp lightly.

Immediately, as each jar is filled, set it in the boiler to process. It is better for two persons to work together, one preparing corn and the other filling jars. If one must work alone, five or six jars are enough to process at one time. Process for four hours.

When canning sweet corn on the cob, follow the same directions, packing the ears whole in the jars. Few jars will hold more than three ears, and this does not make an economical use of jar space.

Egg Plant

Egg plant is more satisfactory as a dried product than canned. After the long processing necessary to kill the bacteria on it, egg plant loses its texture and shape, and becomes a soft, jelly-like substance, difficult to prepare attractively for the table. See last chapter for drying.

Greens: Spinach, Swiss Chard, Kale, Chinese Cabbage Leaves, Dandelions

Blanch 20 minutes over live steam

Plunge until chilled through

Process 2 hours

All greens require careful handling to obtain a satisfactory finished product. Can greens as soon as possible after they are gathered. Pick over carefully, wash and rinse in several changes of fresh cold water, to be sure all grit is removed. A peck of greens is enough to blanch at one time. This will fill a quart jar.

Place the washed greens in a cheesecloth hammock (see page 2), and blanch over live steam for twenty minutes. Plunge immediately in cold water, being careful to give sufficient time so that the chill will permeate to the center of the product. Pack greens closely into hot jars, but do not use any pressure. Add salt, a teaspoon to a quart, and hot water to fill crevices. A teaspoon of olive oil or bacon-fat drippings improves the flavor. Place rubber and cap in position and seal lightly. Process two hours.

Peas

Blanch 5 minutes   Plunge 10 seconds
Process $2\frac{1}{2}$ or 3 hours

Peas should be canned directly after they are brought from the vines, before the sugar in them has had time to change to starch. For satisfactory results, select pods that are well developed and green. After the pods have begun to wither and the peas are hard, it is too late to use them. (See drying of peas, last chapter.)

Shell, blanch for five minutes, plunge, pack in hot jars within one inch of top; add hot water to cover, a teaspoon of salt and a teaspoon of sugar to a quart. Adjust rubber, cover, and clamp lightly. Two and one-half hours' processing is enough for fresh, young peas. Three hours is safer if the peas have been bought or are not strictly fresh-picked.

A cloudy appearance of the liquid in the jar after a few days does not necessarily mean spoilage, but that the peas were carelessly handled, breaking the capsule which incloses the starch, and allowing this to be set free.

If large quantities of peas are picked in the heat, do not allow them to stand in boxes or baskets. The flavor is spoiled by heating while standing in bulk. They should be spread out on tables until shelled, or they will heat through rapidly and be unfit for canning.

Peppers

Omit blanching   Process 2 hours

Sweet green or bullnose peppers are most satisfactory canned, and their use makes a welcome change when the price of fresh peppers is prohibitive. Cut peppers in halves lengthwise, clean out seeds. Pack in hot jars, fitting them in as closely as possible without crushing. Add hot water to cover, and two teaspoons of salt to each quart. Put rubber and cap in position, seal lightly, and process two hours.

To Serve. Chop peppers up in vegetable or meat hash, or fill with corn or tomatoes; add bread crumbs or corn flakes, salt, butter, and paprika. Cook until crumbs are brown. This makes a most appetizing luncheon dish.

Another good combination is to fill peppers with hot cooked rice, add butter or butter substitute, and cover with grated cheese to a depth of one-half inch. Heat in oven until cheese is melted, and serve immediately.

Succotash

Blanch corn 5 minutes   Plunge corn   Process 3 hours

Succotash is a mixture of sweet corn cut from the cob and shelled Lima beans. Its nutritive value is high, and it can be served in place of a meat dish.

Use the same care in canning corn and beans together as when they are canned separately. Pick the vegetables in the morning and can while fresh. Corn should be blanched for five minutes in boiling water, then plunged into cold water. Cut from the cob and mix with equal measure of shelled Lima beans. Pack into freshly washed jars to within one inch of top; add salt, a teaspoon to a quart, and hot water to fill jar. Adjust rubber, cover, and seal lightly. Process three hours.

Summer Squash

Blanch 15 minutes   Plunge 10 seconds   Process 1 hour

Select summer squash before the outside becomes coarse and horny. Wash; cut into slices one inch thick. Put in cheesecloth sack and blanch in boiling water fifteen minutes, to reduce bulk. Plunge into cold water, and pack closely in jars within one inch of top. Add salt, a teaspoon to a quart. The flavor of summer squash is so delicate, that the product is improved if the water used for blanching is added to fill the crevices in the jar, since it contains much of the flavor of the squash. Adjust rubber, cover, and seal lightly. Process one hour.

Tomatoes

Blanch $1\frac{1}{2}$ minutes   Plunge 10 seconds
Process 25 minutes

Select ripe tomatoes and grade for size. Do not use any that are over-ripe or decayed. Wash, put in a cheesecloth sack or wire strainer, and scald for one and one-half minutes to loosen the skins. Plunge. Remove skins and core. Pack directly in hot jars, press down with a wooden spoon, and add one teaspoon of salt to each quart.

Wash bruised or small tomatoes, put in a preserving kettle, skins and all, and cook until soft. Strain through a fine sieve. Return strained liquid to fire, and when hot pour over tomatoes in the jar, within one inch of the top. Adjust rubber, cover, and one clamp. Place in boiler of hot water and process twenty-five minutes. Water should never be added to tomatoes. Jars show shrinkage if poorly packed, or if the strained liquid is not added to fill the crevices, and an unsatisfactory finished product results.

Winter Vegetables

Such vegetables as cabbage, Brussels sprouts, parsnips, squash, pumpkin, onions, potatoes, turnips, and celery keep throughout the winter in dry storage. To put up in glass what will keep in a root cellar adds nothing to the economic life of the nation, and the practice should be discontinued.

Those who live in apartments, and do not have facilities for storing winter vegetables, will find that it is more economical to buy them as needed from local dealers than to can them.

For those who go camping, or on long expeditions into regions where markets are not accessible, it is, no doubt, wise to have on hand a stock of winter as well as summer vegetables which are canned or dried. For instructions in drying of vegetables, see last chapter. For the home canning of winter vegetables, see Farmers' Bulletin 839, which can be had by writing the Department of Agriculture, Washington, D. C.

TIME TABLE FOR VEGETABLES

Do not attempt to use this time table unless familiar with instructions

Product	Blanch	Process
	Minutes	
Asparagus	8 boiling water	$2\frac{1}{2}$ hours
Beans, Baked		$1\frac{1}{2}$ "
Beans, Lima or Shell	Omit blanching	3 "
Beans, String	" "	3 "
Beets	15 boiling water	$2\frac{1}{2}$ "
Carrots	15 " "	$2\frac{1}{2}$ "
Cauliflower	5 boiling water	$1\frac{1}{2}$ "
Corn	5 " "	4 "
Greens (Spinach, Chard, Kale, Dandelions, etc.)	20 over steam	2 "
Peas	5 boiling water	$2\frac{1}{2}$–3 "
Peppers	Omit blanching	2 "
Succotash	See recipe	3 "
Summer Squash	15 boiling water	1 hour
Tomatoes	$1\frac{1}{2}$ " "	25 minutes

Asparagus, Beans (Lima or String), Corn, and Peas should never be canned in any container holding more than a quart.

If pint jars are used, do not vary the time schedule for processing. It is safer to process the same time for pints as for quarts.

Some seasons, the Intermittent Method is indicated for Beans, Corn, and Peas. See page 5.

SOUP MIXTURES

It is well for the thrifty housewife to know the economy of using left-overs from her vegetable canning for soup mixtures. Odds and ends which otherwise might be discarded may be combined and put up in jars. These vegetable combinations are most satisfactory when used with a good meat soup stock, or when used alone for a light soup. Various good mixtures, depending on the individual taste, will occur to the housewife as she works and is guided by the left-overs at hand.

Combinations of tomatoes, beans, peppers, okra, corn, and onions, flavored to taste, can all be used. A pint of vegetable soup mixture added to two pints of clear meat soup stock in the winter makes a good luncheon dish. In packing mixtures, be sure vegetables of strong flavors, like onions, carrots, peppers, etc., are used for piquancy, and not as a foundation.

Follow general directions for all canning. Blanch and plunge each vegetable separately. Then combine, add salt, a teaspoon to a quart, and process the length of time required for the vegetables according to the time schedule. Use the longest processing period given for a vegetable when used alone. When combining corn and tomatoes, however, the acidity of the tomatoes helps to keep the corn, and it is not necessary to process four hours, as is given in the table for the processing time for corn. Two hours is all that is necessary.

Julienne Mixture

After blanching, cut carrots and celery into small cubes. Cut string beans small and add peas. Mix all together. Put into jars, fill within one inch of top with hot water, add salt. Adjust rubber, cover, and seal lightly. Process three hours.

Okra, Corn, and Tomato Mixture

Cut fresh, green okra into thin slices. Blanch for four minutes. Blanch corn five minutes and cut from cob. Measure equal quantities corn and okra, combine, and add three times as much tomatoes, peeled and cut in halves. Mix all together well. Add salt, a teaspoon for each quart, and process two hours.

Tomato, Bean, and Okra Mixture

A good combination is two cups small Lima beans, one quart of strained, thick tomato pulp, and one cup of okra, cut fine. Add sugar, salt, paprika, and onion juice for flavoring. Put in jars and process two hours.

Tomato Soup

Peel tomatoes and boil twenty minutes. Strain through a fine sieve, being sure to get all the pulp. To each pint add two tablespoons of cooked rice, bit of bay leaf, one whole clove, if liked, and salt to taste. Pour into jars and process one and one-half hours.

Concentrated Tomato Soup

Wash ripe tomatoes, cut up and put in a preserve kettle, and cook until tender. Strain through a colander and return to fire, and cook down to one-third the original bulk. Put in jars and proceed according to general directions for canning tomatoes, on page 24.

Tomato Purée

2 quarts thick tomato pulp ½ teaspoonful salt
1 medium-sized onion, chopped 1 teaspoonful sugar
    2 tablespoonsful chopped, sweet red peppers

Tomato purée may be made from small or broken tomatoes. Cut the tomatoes into fourths, and cook them until the pieces become broken and soft. Press the pulp through a sieve, discarding only the seeds and the skins. Add the onion, the pepper pulp, and the seasoning to the strained pulp, and cook the mixture until it is of the consistency of catsup. It is necessary to stir it frequently, in order to keep it from burning. Pour it into jars, adjust rubbers, and seal lightly. Process twenty-five minutes in a hot water bath. Seal, and invert to cool. The purée may be thinned and used for soup or sauce.

CANNING MEAT AND FISH

To preserve meat or fish in glass jars, great care must be exercised. The material must be fresh, the jars carefully washed, and full time must be given for processing.

To prevent all waste in the kitchen, preserve left-over meats, such as chicken, turkey, lamb or beef stew. When a family is small, try preserving what is left over after the second meal, to avoid serving the same kind of meat every day in the week, as is often the case after the Christmas or Thanksgiving turkey. The left-over dishes will be appetizing to the family when served a week or a month later.

The housekeeper who has a flock of hens in the back yard will want to know how to can chicken, so that in the fall, when the roosters are being separated from the pullets, they can be preserved for future use, and not be sold at a sacrifice. One country woman gets two dollars a quart for her canned chicken or roosters. Sold alive, they would net her about eighty cents apiece.

Chicken, Turkey, Duck, or Game

Boil or roast until tender, in the usual way. Remove bones, and cut in pieces to fit into freshly washed jars. If the meat was boiled, add the water in which it was cooked to fill crevices in the jar, after having first boiled it down one-half. For roasted meat, add hot water. Add a teaspoon of salt for a quart, adjust rubber, cover, and seal lightly. Process three hours.

Meat Left-overs: Irish, Lamb, or Beef Stew; Fricassees and Chowder

Put what is left over in carefully washed pint or quart jars. Fill to the top. Adjust rubber, cover, and seal lightly. Process three hours.

Salmon, Mackerel, Halibut, or Trout

Buy fish in season and when the market price is low. Remove head, tail, and backbone. Cut in pieces to fit the jar. Add salt, one teaspoon to a quart, and a little pepper; fill jar with cold water. Adjust rubber, cover, and seal lightly. Process three hours.

The most scrupulous attention to detail is necessary in canning meat and fish, since they spoil so easily. Without such attention results might be serious.

CANNING FRUITS

ALL fruits and berries may be canned successfully without the addition of sugar, simply by adding hot water instead of syrup. As sweetening must be added when the fruit or berries are served, there is no special advantage in omitting it, unless sugar is scarce or high in price. To fruit that is to be used for cooking purposes, such as pie filling, etc., add no sugar.

To can fruit, follow in general the canning instructions for vegetables, using the same equipment. Fruit that is to be preserved must be fresh, of fine flavor, and not over-ripe. When fruit reaches the point of perfect maturity, it begins to change in quality rapidly, and deteriorates.

Blanching and plunging are generally omitted, unless to remove skins, as with peaches; to reduce bulk, as with apples; or to lessen acidity, as with gooseberries, pineapple, and rhubarb.

Use a silver knife for paring fruit, and drop at once into slightly salted cold water, to prevent discoloration. Use two tablespoons of salt to a gallon of fresh cold water. Pack the fruit into clean jars, add syrup or simply hot water. Adjust rubber, cover, and seal lightly. Process the length of time given in the time table.

Syrups

For home canning, a syrup gauge is not necessary to get the right proportion of sugar for fruit. Whether the syrup used is thick or thin is a matter of individual preference, and is not essential to the keeping of the fruits if they are properly processed. The addition of a large amount of sugar spoils rather than improves the flavor. Just enough sugar should be added so that the flavor is brought out and not obscured; moreover, the fruit should be eaten to take the place of fresh fruit in the diet, and not as a sweet preserve.

In judging the amount of syrup to make, it is important to know that large fruits, such as peaches, pears, etc., require just about twice as much syrup to fill the jar as the smaller fruits, owing to the larger spaces between. Well-packed raspberries, blackberries, or strawberries should take but little syrup.

Syrup will keep several days, and it is well to make it a day or two in advance of the actual canning, thereby greatly reducing that day's labor.

The simplest method in making syrups is to have one formula, which is given below. This may be made into a thin, medium, or thick syrup by boiling.

Formula. Put three quarts of sugar and two quarts of water in a preserve kettle, stir until the sugar is dissolved, and bring to the boiling point.

For a **thin syrup,** boil one minute. This syrup is used for sweet cherries, pears, or other fruits when very little sugar is desired.

For a **medium thin syrup,** boil the water and sugar five minutes. This is used for raspberries, strawberries, blackberries, blueberries, etc.

For a **medium thick syrup,** boil the water and sugar ten minutes. This syrup is used for acid fruits, like gooseberries, plums, rhubarb, currants, pineapple, etc.

For a **thick syrup,** boil the water and sugar until it will drop from the side of the spoon in drops. This should be used only for preserves.

Apples *

Do not can the early summer apple. It is better to use this variety as a basis for apple butter or jams. Windfall apples of the fall or winter varieties should be canned for use after the winter apple is out of the market, or when the price is prohibitive. When the apple barrels are picked over, as they should be at least twice during the winter, the apples which are specked or becoming soft may be canned.

Pare and cut out the bruised or soft spots, quarter and core, and drop into slightly salted water. Apples shrink more than most fruits, and it is well to blanch them one minute in boiling water. Plunge into cold water and pack in clean jars. Fill crevices with hot water, adjust rubber, cover, and seal lightly. Process twenty minutes.

Apple Sauce

Windfalls, seconds, or picked-over apples may be made into apple sauce the usual way. Pack hot into clean jars to one-half inch of the top, and process for ten minutes. Have the water just simmering in the hot water bath.

Store jars and use in the spring, when apples are high in price. May be used as pie filling.

Peaches

Select well-ripened peaches. Grade according to size and tie in cheesecloth. Blanch in boiling water just long enough to loosen skins. The length of time will vary from fifteen seconds to one minute, depending on ripeness of fruit. Plunge into cold water and pare with a silver knife. To keep from discoloration, drop pared peaches into slightly salted cold water, using two tablespoons of salt to one gallon of water. Pack into freshly washed jars, whole or halved, with stones removed. Add syrup of desired sweetness, adjust rubber, cover, and seal lightly. Process in hot water bath twenty minutes.

Plums

The yellow egg, green gage, and the common damson plums are used for canning. Stem, and wash in cold water. Do not remove the skins, but prick in several places to keep from bursting. Pack without crushing in freshly washed jars. Fill the jar with syrup of desired sweetness, adjust rubber, cover, and seal lightly. Process for fifteen minutes.

Pears

Follow general directions for apples (page 34), but do not blanch. Small pears may be canned whole. A clove stuck in the end of each pear gives flavor to the fruit. A little lemon peel or thin strips of candied ginger, put in the jar, is pleasing to some tastes. A medium syrup is best for pears. Process twenty minutes.

Pineapple

Pare and core pineapple. Cut in one-inch slices and quarter or leave slices whole, as preferred. Tie in cheesecloth and blanch one minute in boiling water. Plunge into cold water. Pack in jars, fill crevices with thick syrup to one inch of top, adjust rubber, cover, and seal lightly. Process twenty minutes.

Rhubarb

Choose red, juicy stalks. Wash, but do not peel. Cut in one-inch pieces. Tie in cheesecloth, and blanch one minute in boiling water to remove acidity. Plunge into cold water. Pack in jars, fill crevices with thick syrup to one inch of top, adjust rubber, cover, and seal lightly. Process fifteen minutes.

Berries

Blackberries, blueberries, currants, sweet cherries, huckleberries, loganberries, raspberries, and strawberries may all be canned according to these general instructions:

The flavor of canned berries will be better if the sugar is added in the form of syrup before the berries are cooked.

If sugar is scarce or high in price, use water instead of syrup.

Berry juice is sometimes used in place of water to make syrup. This gives to the fruit a darker appearance, and makes a very choice-looking pack.

Do not blanch berries. Pick over carefully, discarding any that are over-ripe or crushed. Remove all stems. Pack in jars, pressing each layer down with a wooden spoon, without crushing fruit. Fill crevices in jar with syrup or water, and process according to time given in time table. See page 39.

If water was added to the berries instead of syrup, when opening the jar, drain the water into a saucepan and boil down one-half. Then add sugar to taste and cook for a few minutes. Pour fruit into hot syrup, boil one minute, and cool before serving.

Sour cherries, cranberries, gooseberries, should be blanched in boiling water for one minute, to reduce their acidity.

Popular Method for Canning Strawberries

If strawberries are packed in jars and syrup added, they rise to the top of the jar and make a poor appearance. The following method is popular, as it gives a good-looking pack:

Pick over strawberries; wash, hull, and put in a deep baking dish. To each quart of berries add one-quarter cup of water and sprinkle well with sugar, using one-half pound of sugar to each quart of berries. Put a cover or plate over the dish, and set in a moderate oven until the berries are soft. When cooked, let stand in the dish in a cool place for twelve hours. Then pack in clean jars to within one-half inch of top, adjust rubber, cover, and seal lightly. Process ten minutes.

Sun-cooked Strawberry Preserve

Do not attempt sun cookery unless hot, dry weather is anticipated. Pick berries early in the morning, wash and hull. Allow equal weights of sugar and fruit. Place the berries on platters in a single layer. Make a thick syrup with sugar, adding just enough berry juice or water to dissolve sugar. Pour over the berries in platters. Cover with a piece of plain window glass and set out of doors in the hot sun for a day or two, depending on weather conditions. The glass should not rest on the berries, but should come a few inches from them. When the berries are soft and the syrup has thickened almost to a jelly, it is time to pack them in freshly washed jars. Adjust rubber, cover, and seal lightly. Put in hot water bath, and have water just simmering for ten minutes. Remove from hot water bath and seal.

Pitted **cherries, raspberries,** and **peaches** may be sun-cooked in the same way as strawberries.

Special Method for Raspberries

Pick over berries carefully, discarding soft ones and any that are wormy. Pack in jars to the brim, pressing each layer down lightly with a wooden spoon. Pour syrup of desired sweetness over berries, and let stand fifteen minutes before sealing. Raspberries have a tendency to settle in the jar, and at the end of fifteen minutes add more berries. Adjust rubber and cover, seal lightly, and process fifteen minutes.

TIME TABLE FOR FRUITS AND BERRIES WITH KIND OF SYRUP TO USE

Do not attempt to use this table until familiar with General Canning Instructions (pages 1 and 32)

Fruit	Blanch	Process	Syrup
	Minute	Minutes	
Apples	1	20	Water instead
Blackberries	Omit	15	Medium
Blueberries or	Omit	15	Medium
Huckleberries	Omit	15	Thin
Cherries (sweet)	Omit	18	Medium
Cherries (sour)	1	18	Thick
Cranberries	1	15	Thick
Currants	Omit	15	Thick
Gooseberries	1	15	Thick
Loganberries	Omit	15	Medium
Peaches	1	20	Thick
Pears	Omit	20	Medium
Pineapple	1	20	Thick
Plums	Omit	15	Thick
Raspberries	Omit	15	Medium
Rhubarb	1	15	Thick
Strawberries	Omit	10	Medium

Remember that in case of sugar shortage water may be added to the fruit in place of syrup, and the sweetening added when the jar is opened.

Unless fruits or berries are to be used for pie filling, when water is used in place of syrup do not discard it. Drain, boil down one-half, then add sugar to make a syrup of desired sweetness. Pour berries or fruit into hot syrup and cook a few minutes. Cool before serving.

COLD WATER METHOD FOR PRESERVING FRUIT

CRANBERRIES, gooseberries, rhubarb, can be kept for winter use without cooking, by the cold water process. A few general rules should be observed.

Cranberries. Pick over and remove stems. Be sure all soft ones are discarded, or they will ferment and spoil all. Wash the berries and pack in freshly washed jars. Adjust new rubber. Put jar filled with cranberries in deep pail, and turn in clean cold water. When the water in the pail comes over the top of the jar five or six inches, put on cover and *seal under water*.

Gooseberries. Select gooseberries before they begin to turn red, and do not break the capsules which inclose pulp and seed of the berries. The greatest care must be exercised in picking over the berries, that no soft ones are used, or they will ferment, spoiling the contents. Follow general directions for cranberries, sealing under water.

Rhubarb. Wash before cutting. Do not remove skin. Cut in inch pieces, or leave in lengths to fit the jars. Follow general directions for cranberries, sealing under water.

To Serve. The following is considered the most satisfactory of the many methods of preparing rhubarb that has been kept in cold water: Do not throw away the water in the jar. Pour into a kettle and boil down until one-half the original amount. Add the rhubarb, cook until soft, and add sugar to taste. Orange peel or a slice of lemon cooked in the liquid greatly improves the flavor for some tastes.

JELLY MAKING

JELLY making is simple enough, if a few general rules are observed. Those who wish to know the scientific principles underlying the art are referred to "Successful Canning and Preserving," by Ola Powell, and to "The Principles of Jelly Making," by N. E. Goldthwaite, Ph.D. The latter is a free bulletin (No. 31), issued by the University of Illinois, Urbana, Illinois.

Jellies are made by cooking together certain fruit juices and sugar in the right proportion. A good jelly will have certain essential qualities. It should be of good color, with sparkling transparency, of decided flavor, and firm enough, without being tough or gummy, to hold its shape when slipped out of the glass.

Fruit juice is composed mostly of water, and also of small amounts of flavoring substance, sugar, acids, and a most important substance called **pectin**. Without pectin present in the fruit juice, no jelly can be made unless artificial means are employed. Some fruits are very rich in pectin, while others have very little; hence the importance of choosing fruit rich in pectin, or of combining two fruits when a fruit is known to have but little pectin. Sour apples, unripe grapes, currants, and quinces have a large proportion of pectin; while pears, peaches, strawberries, and cherries have smaller amounts. Over-ripe fruit is almost entirely deficient in pectin, and it is impossible to make jelly from it. Always cook fruit before straining out the juice, for heat is essential in developing the pectin. Uncooked fruit is often found lacking in pectin, while the same fruit cooked is found to have a great deal.

In using another fruit juice to supply pectin, use equal measure of the two juices. Apples are ordinarily used for this purpose, since apple juice is mild, and will not obscure the desired flavor. Grapes and quinces have too decided a flavor of their own to be used as a pectin supply.

To discover whether fruit juice has pectin, take a little of the juice on a saucer and add to it a small amount of grain alcohol, ninety-five per cent pure. If a gelatinous mass forms, there is enough pectin in the juice to make a good jelly. If there is no pectin, the juice must be cooked again with apple parings, apple juice, or the white inner skin of lemons, oranges, or grapefruit. Continue the cooking of the fruit juice until it responds to the alcohol or pectin test.

Failures in jelly making are usually attributable to four causes: Use of over-ripe fruit; use of too much sugar; cooking too large a quantity of fruit juice at a time; failure to add a fruit rich in pectin when using fruits known to be lacking in pectin, as, for example, using ripe cherries without combining with their juice some apple juice, to supply pectin.

General Rules to Follow in Making Jelly

One secret of quick and perfect jelly is to have everything **hot** which comes in contact with the jelly. Add the sugar after heating it (on a platter in the oven is often the most convenient way), and have the jelly glasses standing in hot water, ready for the jelly as soon as it is ready to take from the stove. Have everything at hand before putting the fruit juice to boil.

With a wooden potato masher or spoon, crush **soft fruit**, such as raspberries, strawberries, grapes, etc., in a saucepan, add just enough water to prevent burning, and heat slowly over the fire. When hot throughout (do not let fruit boil) pour into a jelly bag and let drip. The jelly bag may be suspended from the backs of two chairs, or in any clean and convenient place where it will be out of the way.

Hard fruits, such as apples, quinces, peaches, plums, pears, etc., are prepared for jelly making as follows: Wash; do not remove skins; cut up and put in a saucepan, cores, seeds, and all. Barely cover with water and cook until soft. Drain in a jelly bag until the pulp is dry. Do not press the bag. Four to six hours is usually long enough to let fruit drain.

To make a **second extraction,** return the pulp from the jelly bag to the saucepan, add enough water to prevent burning, and heat through. Return to the jelly bag and let drip. This second extraction may be combined with the first, if desired. The alcohol test for pectin will show whether the second extraction will make jelly, or be fit only for fruit juice.

To make a good jelly, fruit juice should taste about as tart as a sour apple. If juice is found to be lacking in acidity, add a little lemon or other acid fruit juice. The addition of acidity improves not only the flavor, but the texture of the jelly. This is true of jelly made from flavorless apples, quinces, blackberries, and blueberries.

Jelly pulp may be cooked with a little water, spices and sugar added to taste, and made into a fruit butter.

Measure the fruit juice before putting it over the heat, bring to the boiling point quickly, and boil eight minutes. Skim just before adding the sugar, and then as needed.

To each quart of juice add three-fourths of a quart of **sugar** which has been heated. There are three exceptions to this general rule, blueberries, green grapes, and currants. With these juices allow equal measures of sugar. Stir until the sugar is dissolved, then boil rapidly from three to five minutes.

Make jelly in **small quantities.** One quart or three pints of fruit juice is enough to make into jelly at one time. Such quantities can be handled more safely and successfully. If one desires to make more jelly, have two saucepans over the fire, with a quart of juice in each.

The most reliable and the simplest **test** by which to know when to take jelly from the stove is called the two-drop test. A little experience in this method gives one a safe guide for all time. Take a little of the boiling syrup on a tablespoon, after the sugar has been cooked in it for three minutes, and pour the syrup from the side of the spoon above the kettle. When the jelly is done, the syrup will form in two large, thick drops at the side of the spoon before falling off. Remove at once from the fire and pour into jelly glasses, which should be standing in hot water.

A single layer of damp cheesecloth placed over the top of the glass may be used as a strainer, in case some of the white coating from the sides of the saucepan is floating in the jelly.

Jelly may be made on a rainy or cloudy day, as well as when the sun shines brightly.

If jelly does not seem firm enough after it is cold, let it stand for a few days in the hot sun, covered by a piece of plain window glass.

Honey may be used in place of sugar, with equal measures of fruit juice and honey.

Give great care to the **jelly bag,** especially those made of felt. See that the bag is scalded and hung out of doors in the sun after use. Any sourness about the jelly bag imparts a flat, insipid taste to the fruit juice. Fruits are sometimes blamed for their lack of good flavor, when a poorly cared for jelly bag is really the cause.

When making jelly in the winter, it is well to let the fruit drip from the jelly bag near a hot stove or radiator. The pectin in the fruit juice causes the bag to stiffen when it is cold, and if the fruit becomes chilled, a great deal of the juice is lost in this way.

To Cover Jelly

When the jelly is cold, melt a little paraffin in a saucepan and pour over the top. Be sure that the paraffin touches the edge of the glass all around. A tablespoon of melted paraffin is enough to cover and protect the jelly. Great, thick coverings of paraffin are unnecessary and wasteful. Tip the glass after putting on the paraffin, in order that it will reach the edges all around. Another method is to cut white paper to fit the glass above the jelly. Dip the paper in brandy before putting on top of the jelly. Either of these methods will protect jelly indefinitely. When jelly is for immediate use, the brandy is superfluous.

Apple Jelly

Wipe apples, remove stems, but do not peel. Cut out any imperfect spots. Quarter and put in porcelain-lined or agate kettle, barely cover with water, and cook until tender. Mash and drain through a colander, then drain this juice in a jelly bag. The apple may be put at once into the bag, but if convenient to use the colander first, the draining is quicker. Proceed according to general instructions, page 43. If the color of the fruit juice is light, a little red vegetable coloring matter may be added just before removing the jelly from the stove. Use about as much coloring matter as one might pick up on the point of a penknife for each pint of juice.

To vary the above recipe, just before turning the jelly into the hot glasses, add a teaspoon of vanilla extract or a teaspoon of almond extract to a quart of juice, or hold a lemon verbena or rose geranium leaf in the hot jelly for a few seconds. Each of these gives to the jelly quite a decided flavor, thought delicious by many. A thin slice of lemon or orange cooked in the juice before the sugar is added, and then removed, is helpful, especially when the apples are not of good acidity.

Spiced Apple Jelly

Into one quart of apple juice, measured before setting to boil and before the sugar is added, put a spice bag of fine muslin containing one-half teaspoon of clove and one teaspoon of cinnamon. Cook in the juice five minutes. Remove just before the sugar is added. Add sugar and proceed according to general directions, page 44.

Apple Jelly from Parings

Thrifty housewives have long been familiar with the delicious jelly made from apple parings. When making apple pies, save the parings, seeds, and cores of the apples. Put in a saucepan and cover with cold water. Cook until parings are soft and have lost their color. Strain through a sieve and put the juice to drip in the jelly bag. Proceed as for apple jelly, page 45. The parings from enough apples to make two apple pies will give one tumbler of jelly. The color from the parings gives a deep crimson jelly, which is really a first quality product, made from what is so often thrown into the garbage.

Crabapple Jelly

Choose sound, well-colored apples. Cut in halves and proceed as for apple jelly, page 45.

Barberry Jelly

Pick barberries before the frost touches them.

To four quarts of apples, cut up, add three pints of barberries. Add water barely to cover the fruit, and cook until the barberries are shriveled. Strain through a jelly bag and proceed according to general instructions, page 43.

Blueberry Jelly

Quite uncommon is the delicious jelly made from the blueberry. Extract the juice in the usual way, as for all soft berries, page 42. Drain in the jelly bag. Two and even three extractions can be made from the pulp. Proceed according to general directions, using equal measures of sugar and juice. This gives a sweet rather than an acid jelly. A little lemon juice added before removing from the stove improves the flavor.

Cranberry Jelly

Take three half-pints of apple juice and one half-pint cranberry juice, measured after it has dripped through the jelly bag. Heat three-fourths the combined measure of sugar, and add to the juice after it has boiled five minutes. Proceed according to general instructions, page 44.

Currant Jelly

Do not pick currants directly after a rain, as they take up a great deal of moisture. Equal proportions of red and white currants may be used, making a jelly much lighter in color than when all red currants are used. Do not remove the stems from the currants. Wash and drain. Put in a porcelain or agate kettle, and mash with a wooden masher. Cook until the currants have lost their color. Strain through a colander and put juice to drip through a jelly bag. Measure, and proceed as for all jelly making, page 43, but use equal measures of sugar and juice. Three extractions of juice for jelly may be made from currants.

Another method that saves the work of different extractions is to cover the currants with water at first. The cooking then extracts all the juice at once.

Elderberry Jelly
Contributed by Mrs. Bates

Pick elderberries when they are red, just before turning dark. Use two parts of elderberries to one part apples. Pick the elderberries from the stems, quarter the apples, and cook together until soft. Strain through a jelly bag. Boil the juice three to five minutes, and add three-fourths the measure of heated sugar. Proceed according to general directions, page 44.

Grape Jelly

Do not use grapes which are fully ripened. They are best for jelly when some still red are mixed with the purple ones. Grapes should be picked over, washed, and the stems removed before putting into white-lined or agate saucepan. Put over the fire, mash with a pestle, and let simmer very gently until softened throughout. Pour into a jelly bag and let drip over night. Proceed as for all jellies, page 43.

Green Grape Jelly

Pick the grapes just before they take on color. Follow instructions for grape jelly, but use equal measures of sugar and juice. A little green vegetable coloring paste may be necessary to give an attractive color. Add just before removing the jelly from the stove.

Mint Jelly

Proceed as for apple jelly, page 45. Three minutes before removing from the stove, add the crushed leaves and stalks of a small bunch of mint. When the jelly is ready to pour, take out the mint and add a little green vegetable coloring paste. Strain the jelly through a cheesecloth spread over the glasses, or tied tightly about the saucepan; otherwise bits of mint leaf may be floating in the jelly and spoil its transparency.

Quince Jelly

Proceed as for apple jelly, page 45, using quinces in place of apples and removing the seeds from fruit before cooking. Quince parings make delicious jelly, while the better portions may be used for preserves, etc.

Raspberry Jelly

Raspberries must not be too ripe. Combine equal measures of apple juice with raspberry juice, and after boiling ten minutes add three-fourths the combined measure of heated sugar. Proceed as for all jellies, page 44.

Raspberry juice may be combined with strawberry juice.

Strawberry Jelly

Strawberry juice contains but little pectin, therefore apple juice must be added in order to make a satisfactory jelly. As apples are not in season when strawberries are ripe, store the strawberry juice (page 53) in jars until the fall. Prepare apple juice in the usual way, and add two parts apple juice to one part strawberry juice, and proceed according to general directions, page 43.

Triple Fruit Jelly

Boil together, until soft, four quinces, pared and cut small, one quart of cranberries, two quarts of apples, cut up. Strain through a jelly bag over night. Measure the juice and boil three to five minutes. Add an equal measure of heated sugar, and boil from three to ten minutes. Test by the two-drop method. Pour in hot glasses.

FRUIT JUICES

No preserve closet is complete without a good supply of fruit juice, stored to use for jelly making, for desserts, or for beverages. Many housekeepers make their fruit juices in season, and instead of spending their time in the kitchen when it is fine weather, leave jelly making until cold or stormy days. Some housekeepers, too, prefer their jelly made fresh, and keep on hand a generous supply of fruit juices, which can be made up into jelly as needed, six or eight glasses at a time.

Apple, blackberry, cherry, currant, grape, raspberry, and strawberry juice can be used in a variety of ways other than in jelly making. Nothing is more palatable on a hot day than a cold drink which can be made easily from bottled fruit juice. The addition of cracked ice, a slice of lemon, and sugar or syrup to taste, makes an inviting beverage, served in place of the customary afternoon tea. Economical desserts, also, such as sherbets and a variety of gelatine dishes, may be made from fruit juices.

Use the same care in selecting and washing fruits and berries for making fruit juices that you would for preserving or jelly making. Green or unripe fruit is not desirable, since its acidity is too great, while over-ripe fruit imparts a disagreeable flavor to the juice. Therefore it is important to choose only ripe, perfect fruit, if a first quality fruit juice is desired.

Extract the juice from the berries or fruit as if jelly were to be made, page 42. In heating the fruit, always use a porcelain or agate kettle, adding just enough water to keep from burning. Crush with a wooden masher, and when hot throughout put into the jelly bag to drip. Do not let the fruit boil before removing from the fire. Heating the fruit increases the yield of juice, and gives a better flavor and color to the product. Never add sugar to fruit juice which is to be made into jelly. It may be used in juices stored for beverages, desserts, etc., but with no special advantage.

Bottling. Pour the fruit juice which has dripped from the jelly bag into sterilized bottles or jars, to within one inch of top. (Boil the bottles or jars for ten minutes before adding the fruit juice, since it is not to be sterilized.) The space between the juice and the top of the bottles allows for expansion when the juice is hot.

Have new corks to fit the bottles, soaking in warm soda water (a teaspoon of soda to a quart of water) for thirty minutes. Rinse well in boiling water before using. Put the corks loosely in the bottles before putting them into the hot water bath. A piece of cloth tied over the cork will keep it in place and prevent its blowing out during the processing. If juices are stored in jars, fill to one-half inch of the top, adjust rubber, cap, and seal lightly.

Processing. Fruit juices are *pasteurized* rather than sterilized. This means that the temperature of the hot water bath should be kept below boiling, or just at the simmering point. The wash boiler can be used in pasteurizing as well as in sterilizing. Be sure to put racks in the bottom of the boiler before putting in bottles or jars.

Have the water in the boiler come to within one inch of the top of the bottles or jars. Heat the water quickly, and keep simmering for twenty minutes. Do not begin to count the time until the water is seen to be at the simmering point. No harm is done if the water boils for a minute or two, but the juice has a better color if the bath is kept just below the boiling point.

Sealing. Remove the bottles or jars from the container, and if bottles are used, press the corks firmly in as far as they will go, and set aside to cool. When the bottles are cool, dip the cork and end of the neck of the bottle into melted paraffin, to make an air-tight seal.

If jars are used, seal completely, in the usual way.

A white sediment will sometimes form in the bottom of the bottle or jar. This does not indicate that the juice has spoiled; simply that acid crystals have settled. In jelly making, care should be used, in pouring juice from the bottle, that this sediment is not disturbed; otherwise the jelly will not be clear.

For those who wish to bottle fruit juice for commercial purposes, Miss Ola Powell's "Successful Canning and Preserving" is recommended.

All fruit juices are made and bottled in the same general way, and it will not be necessary for the housewife to have detailed directions to follow for each kind of fruit. Directions for strawberry juice are given in full, as a guide for the other fruit juices.

Strawberry Juice

Select well ripened strawberries. Put in a colander, and wash all grit from the fruit; then hull. Put the berries in a porcelain or agate kettle; add enough water to keep the fruit from scorching; mash with a wooden masher until the berries are soft. Leave over the fire until the berries are heated throughout. Do not let boil. Put to drain in jelly bag. Bottle according to general directions. Pasteurize for twenty minutes.

Grape Juice

A simple method

10 pounds grapes   Sugar

Pick ten pounds of grapes from stems, and wash. Simmer until soft in two quarts of water. Mash through a colander, and drain over night in a jelly bag. To one quart of fruit juice add one-half cup of sugar. Bring to the boiling point, pour in hot sterilized jars, and process eight minutes.

Raspberry Vinegar

4 quarts raspberries   1 quart vinegar
6 cups sugar

Put half the berries in a large bowl; add the vinegar, and let stand over night. Strain, and squeeze well through cheesecloth. Pour this juice over the other half of the berries, and let stand over night. Squeeze, and strain the liquid; add sugar and bring to the boiling point. Seal air-tight. This may be used in fruit punches in the summer, or as a drink, diluted with water.

Dandelion Shrub

2 quarts dandelion blossoms   3 lemons
4 quarts boiling water   3 oranges
4 pounds white sugar   ¾ cake compressed yeast

Pour boiling water over the blossoms. Let stand on the back of the stove twenty-four hours. Slice lemons and oranges thin, remove seeds; pour sugar over them, and let stand over night. Strain blossoms from water, and pour the strained liquid over orange, lemon, and sugar. Add yeast dissolved in a little lukewarm water. Let the mixture stand five or six days, with cheesecloth for covering. Skim when necessary. Then strain again, and bottle.

Two typical recipes for the use of fruit juices are given. Every housekeeper can make her own adaptations.

Grape or Raspberry Tapioca

3 cups grape or raspberry juice $\frac{1}{2}$ cup sugar
$\frac{1}{2}$ cup minute tapioca

Heat the grape or raspberry juice; add one-half cup of minute tapioca and one-half cup of sugar. Cook for fifteen minutes in a double boiler. Chill, and serve with whipped cream.

Grape Juice Sherbet

1 pint grape juice $1\frac{1}{2}$ cups boiling water
4 tablespoons lemon juice $\frac{1}{2}$ cup cold water
Juice of half an orange 1 cup sugar
1 tablespoon granulated gelatine

Soak gelatine in cold water five minutes. Make a syrup by boiling the sugar and hot water for fifteen minutes; then add the soaked gelatine. Cool slightly; add grape, orange, and lemon juice. Freeze, using a mixture of three parts ice to one of salt.

PICKLING

PICKLING is preserving with salt or vinegar. In adding spices and condiments to pickles, one may be guided by individual taste. Some prefer pickles highly spiced, while others wish for very little seasoning.

Equipment. Only porcelain-lined or agate kettles should be used when cooking pickles. Acids attack metal utensils and spoil the pickles. Use a wooden spoon for stirring.

Jars should be well washed and scalded before being used. Rubbers which come with the jars may be used in place of new ones for sealing pickles.

Sealing. All pickles should be sealed air-tight. Ordinarily it is not necessary to process them in the hot water bath after partial sealing.

Brine. When recipe calls for brine, make as follows: one cup of salt to four quarts of water.

FAVORITE RECIPES FROM OLD NEW ENGLAND FAMILIES

Pickled String Beans

Contributed by a Sherborn farmer

Select tender beans, fresh from the garden. Do not break off ends or string. Leave whole, and wash in cold water. Spread on the table to dry. Take a large crock; sprinkle a layer of salt in the bottom of the crock to a depth of one inch. When the beans are dry, put in a layer of beans, then a generous handful of salt. Alternate layers of beans with salt until crock is full. Cover well with salt. Put large plate on top and weigh down with heavy stone. Beans will keep this way all winter.

To Use. Take out beans as needed. Wash. Remove ends, string and cut up. Put into boiling hot water and boil rapidly for fifteen minutes. Pour off water, add fresh boiling water, and cook until tender.

Pickled Beets

Cook young beets in an open kettle until soft. Plunge into cold water and slip off the skins with the fingers. Pack into jars. Fill jars with weak solution of vinegar and water. Adjust rubber, cap, seal lightly, and process one hour. Equal parts of vinegar and water give good flavor to the beets. If the vinegar is old and strong, use one part vinegar to two parts water.

Pickled Corn

Blanch corn on the cob in boiling water for three minutes. Plunge into cold water and cut from the cob. Pack into a small stone crock, and add one cup of salt to every nine cups of corn. Mix thoroughly. Put plate on top of corn and hold down with a heavy weight. After a few days, brine from the corn should form over the rim of the plate. If not, add brine made from one-half cup of salt to one quart of cold water. Pour into the crock to cover the plate.

To Use. Take out the amount of corn needed, putting the plate in place again. Rinse in cold water. Cover corn with plenty of water, and bring to the boil. Then pour off the water. Repeat this process. Drain through a colander and put in the oven to dry out. It is now ready to serve. Add milk, butter or butter substitute, and seasoning.

Celery Pickle

Contributed by Miss Ida Putnam

- 3 pints chopped green tomatoes
- 3 pints chopped ripe tomatoes
- 2½ pints chopped onions
- 2 bunches celery, chopped with leaves
- 2 medium-sized red peppers

Do not peel tomatoes. Mix all together, add one-half cup salt, and let stand over night. Drain and add:

- 2 quarts vinegar
- 1 quart sugar
- ½ teaspoon cinnamon
- ½ teaspoon cloves
- ½ cup mustard seed

Cook twenty minutes or more. Seal in jars.

Canned Cucumbers

Miss Stockin's recipe

Peel fresh cucumbers, cut in one-quarter inch slices, and soak in brine for eight hours. Drain well and pack into jars. Fill the jars with vinegar, stirring the cucumbers with a fork, that the liquid may fill all crevices. When the jars are full, seal lightly and put in boiler, with warm water to come over the top of the jars. Bring water to the boiling point and boil for fifteen minutes. Remove and seal.

Pickled Cucumbers

Cut small cucumbers from the vine, leaving one-half inch of stem. Wash carefully, rubbing off all the little, prickly black spots. Pack jars full. Add one teaspoon of salt and one-fourth teaspoon of cayenne pepper to each quart. Fill jars to overflowing with cold vinegar, adjust new rubber, and seal tight.

Uncooked Cucumber Pickle

10 medium-sized cucumbers   1 tablespoon celery seed
2 small onions   2 tablespoons mustard seed
½ pint white wine vinegar   ½ cup olive oil

Pare and slice cucumbers thin. Sprinkle with one-half cup salt and let stand over night. In the morning, place in colander and rinse off the salt. Drain; add onions, chopped fine, and other ingredients. Mix all together well. Seal in jars. This recipe makes about three pints.

Chopped Pickle

4 quarts green tomatoes   1 cup salt
1 quart onions   1 cup white mustard seed
18 large green peppers   1 cup celery seed
12 large red peppers   4 quarts vinegar
4 quarts cabbage   2 pounds brown sugar

Remove seeds from peppers. Chop tomatoes, onions, cabbage, and peppers; add one cup of salt, and mix well. Cover with water and let stand over night. In the morning, drain.

Boil vinegar and sugar for twenty minutes. Pour over drained vegetables, add mustard and celery seed, and cook until tomatoes are soft. Seal while hot.

Mustard Pickle

2 bunches celery   6 teaspoons mustard
2 heads cauliflower   1 tablespoon turmeric powder
2 small red peppers   2 cups sugar
1 qt. small silver-skin onions   1 cup flour
2½ quarts vinegar

Cut celery in inch pieces, break cauliflower in flowerets. Remove seeds from peppers, and chop fine. Peel onions.

Combine all vegetables and put in brine for twenty-four hours. Then cook in the same brine until tender. Drain.

Mix dry ingredients with water, to make a smooth paste; add vinegar, boiling hot, and cook until creamy. Pour over vegetables. Cook all together for a few minutes. Seal in jars. This will keep two years.

Philadelphia Pickle

12 ripe tomatoes	½ cup raisins
2 large peppers	1 cup brown sugar
2 large onions	1 cup vinegar
1 stalk celery	1 tablespoon salt
Cinnamon and cloves to taste	

Peel and quarter tomatoes. Remove seeds from peppers, and chop peppers, onions, and celery fine. Combine vegetables and cook ten minutes. Add spices; bring to the boiling point; add raisins and sugar, and cook until tomatoes and onions are soft. Seal hot in jars.

Green Tomato Pickle

½ peck green tomatoes	3 cups brown sugar
1 quart onions	1 ounce mustard seed
2 red peppers	1 ounce celery seed
4 green sweet peppers	Vinegar (see directions)
Spice bag containing 12 whole cloves, handful stick cinnamon, and teaspoon allspice	

Slice tomatoes and onions thin. Sprinkle with one cup of salt, and let stand over night. In the morning, drain and rinse off the salt. Remove seeds from peppers and chop peppers fine. Put all in a kettle and just cover with vinegar. Add spice bag, and cook until vegetables are soft. Remove bag; add sugar, mustard seed, celery seed, and cook ten minutes more. Seal in jars.

Dutch Salad

4 quarts green tomatoes
1½ quarts button onions
1 quart cucumber pickles
1 head cauliflower
1 bunch celery

6 green sweet peppers
6 teaspoons mustard
1 tablespoon turmeric powder
2 cups sugar
1 cup flour

2½ quarts vinegar

Chop tomatoes and peppers fine. Break cauliflower into flowerets, discarding only the leaves. Discard leaves of celery, cut stalks into inch pieces. Peel onions. Combine all vegetables, with the exception of the cucumber pickles. Cover with brine and let stand twenty-four hours. Then boil in the same brine for thirty minutes, and drain. To cooked vegetables add cucumber pickles, cut in half-inch cubes.

Mix dry ingredients with water, to form a smooth paste. Add vinegar, boiling hot, and cook until creamy. Pour over well-drained vegetables. Cook a few minutes. Seal air-tight. This will keep two or three years.

Sweet Pickled Cherries

3 quarts red or black cherries
3 cups vinegar

2 pounds sugar
¼ teaspoon ground clove

½ teaspoon cinnamon

Remove cherry pits. Combine vinegar, sugar, and spices, and cook until syrup is thick. Pour over cherries and simmer for three minutes. Let stand over night and cook again, boiling gently for ten minutes. Seal in jars.

Sweet Pickled Crabapples

7 pounds crabapples   1 quart vinegar
1 pint water   3 pounds sugar
2 tablespoons whole cloves

Boil sugar, water, and vinegar ten minutes. Add cloves and crabapples. Cook until apples are tender, but not soft. Pack into jars. Cook syrup until thick, and fill crevices between apples with hot syrup. Seal air-tight.

Ripe Cucumber Pickle

10 large, ripe cucumbers   1 quart vinegar
2 pounds sugar   Spice bag

Pare and seed large, ripe cucumbers. Cut each cucumber lengthwise into four pieces. Let stand twenty-four hours, covered with vinegar, in a cool place. Drain.

Boil two pounds of sugar and one quart of vinegar for twenty minutes, with spice bag containing two teaspoons cinnamon and one of clove. Remove bag. Add drained cucumbers, and cook in syrup until tender. When soft, pack cucumbers in hot jars. Cinnamon stick may be added to the jars when packing. Cook syrup down until thick enough to jell on a saucer, and pour hot over cucumbers. Seal. This is delicious if kept six months before opening.

Sweet Marlborough Pickle

8 pickled limes (commercial variety)
12 green tomatoes
¾ pound of sugar to every pound of mixture

Remove seeds from limes, and chop limes fine with the tomatoes. (Do not throw away any of the lime juice.) Add sugar and cook two hours. As mixture thickens, add juice from limes, to keep from burning. Seal in glasses and cover with paraffin.

Sweet Peach Pickle

8 pounds peaches 1 teaspoon allspice
4 pounds brown sugar 1 teaspoon cassia buds
1 quart vinegar 6 whole cloves
Stick cinnamon (4 good-sized pieces)

Put spices in bag. Make syrup of sugar and vinegar. Add spice bag, and cook until syrup is thick. Peel and stone peaches, if desired. Cook in syrup until soft. Remove peaches from syrup without breaking, put into jars, and pour syrup over them. Next day, drain off syrup; boil again until thick, and return to peaches. Repeat process three days. This will keep in a stone crock.

Pickled Watermelon Rind
A simple method

Watermelon rind 5 pounds sugar
Vinegar 2 ounces whole mace
2 ounces whole clove

Pare the rind of a watermelon. (Do not use pink part of melon.) Cut in one-inch pieces, and let stand in diluted vinegar—equal parts vinegar and water—to cover, for twelve hours. Boil until tender in same solution. Then drain well.

For a syrup, use five pounds sugar to one quart vinegar. Put in a preserving kettle, and add spice bag containing two ounces whole mace, two ounces whole clove. Boil for five minutes. Put in melon rind and cook a few minutes. Remove rind from syrup and put into hot jars, being careful not to break pieces. Boil syrup down until thick, pour over rind in jars, and seal while hot.

Cranberry Ketchup

5 pounds cranberries
1 pint vinegar
2 pounds brown sugar
½ tablespoon paprika
3 tablespoons cinnamon
½ tablespoon ground clove
½ tablespoon salt

Cook cranberries and vinegar until cranberries are soft. Strain, add other ingredients, and cook until thick. While hot, seal in jars.

Gooseberry Ketchup

6 quarts green or ripe gooseberries
9 pounds white sugar
1 pint vinegar
1 tablespoon each cinnamon and allspice
1 teaspoon clove

Pick the blooms off the berries. Put one-half the sugar in a kettle; add berries, vinegar, and cook one and one-half hours. Add remaining sugar, spices, and cook one-half hour longer. Seal in jars while hot.

Grape Ketchup

An old Scotch recipe

10 pounds grapes
5 pounds sugar
1 quart cider vinegar
2 tablespoons cinnamon
2 tablespoons allspice
2 tablespoons cloves

Pick over grapes, wash; cook in porcelain-lined kettle until soft. Mash, put through a sieve, add sugar and spices, and boil twenty minutes. Add vinegar, boil fifteen minutes, and bottle while hot.

Tomato Ketchup

½ bushel ripe tomatoes   ¼ pound whole cloves
1 quart onions   1 quart sugar
3 red sweet peppers   1 cup salt
¼ pound allspice buds   1 quart vinegar
¼ teaspoon cayenne

Choose only well ripened tomatoes, without green or yellow spots. Small or broken fruit, or extra juice left over from canning, may be used with whole tomatoes. Boiling should be done as rapidly as possible in an enameled or porcelain-lined kettle. Since ground spices darken the product, whole spices should be used.

Put tomatoes, skins and all, in kettle. Mash with wooden masher. Remove seeds from peppers; add peppers and onions, chopped fine. Then add whole spices, and cook until tomatoes are well done. Strain through a sieve, leaving nothing but skins, seeds, and spices in the strainer. To the strained liquid add the sugar, salt, vinegar, and cayenne. Boil rapidly until reduced one-third. Cool, and bottle in freshly washed bottles. Dip corks in melted paraffin, and seal.

Governor Sauce
From Jamaica

1 peck green tomatoes   3 onions
1½ cups brown sugar   2 red peppers
Vinegar (see directions)
Spice bag containing 12 whole cloves, ¼ cup
  celery seed, 1 teaspoon mace, 1 teaspoon
  black pepper, and a bay leaf

Slice tomatoes, sprinkle with one cup of salt, and let stand over night. In the morning, drain well and rinse off the salt. Seed peppers, chop fine; add tomatoes, onions sliced thin, sugar, and spice bag. Cover with vinegar and boil gently three hours. Seal in jars while hot.

Sweet Indian Chutney

4 cups chopped sour apples
4 cups chopped raisins
10 ripe tomatoes
¼ pound preserved ginger
3 pounds light brown sugar
½ pound white mustard seed
1 shallot or 1 onion
½ cup salt
1 quart strong vinegar
¼ teaspoon cayenne pepper

Peel and quarter tomatoes. Combine all ingredients and cook gently about three hours. Watch carefully as mixture thickens, since it will burn easily. Seal in jars.

Peach Chuddy

Unusual old recipe

3 hard, unripe peaches
5 large apples
1 large Spanish onion
1 red sweet pepper
1 pound seeded raisins
1 pound dried currants
2 pounds brown sugar
1 quart vinegar
2 teaspoons ginger
2 teaspoons cinnamon
2 teaspoons salt
½ teaspoon clove

Peel and quarter peaches and apples. Peel onions and remove seeds from peppers. Combine all and chop fine. Add other ingredients, with the exception of spices, and cook one hour. Then add spices, cook ten minutes, and seal in glasses. Cover with paraffin.

Tomato Cream

1 dozen ripe tomatoes | ¼ pound mustard
1 dozen large onions | 1 pound brown sugar
1 dozen apples | 1 teaspoon cayenne pepper
1 tablespoon salt

Peel tomatoes, onions, and apples, and chop fine. Boil until very soft, and strain through a wire sieve. When nearly cold, add other ingredients. Boil until thick, and bottle hot. Seal with cork dipped in melted paraffin.

Bordeaux Relish
Contributed by Miss Ida Putnam

½ peck green tomatoes | 2 red peppers
3 onions | ½ cup salt
3 quarts vinegar | 1 cup sugar
2 ounces white mustard seed | 2 dozen whole cloves
2 ounces celery seed | 2 dozen whole allspice
2 small white cabbages
(size of a large grapefruit)

Chop cabbage, tomatoes, onions, and peppers. Put in hot vinegar and cook one hour or more. Add spices twenty minutes before taking from the stove.

Cape Cod Pepper Relish

1 dozen green sweet peppers | 1 quart vinegar
1 dozen red sweet peppers | 2½ cups sugar
1 dozen medium-sized onions | 2 tablespoons salt

Cut up peppers and remove seeds. Peel onions, and put onions and peppers through the meat grinder. Cover with boiling water and let stand for five minutes. Drain.

Cover again with boiling water and let stand ten minutes. Drain again. Add sugar, vinegar, salt, and boil fifteen minutes. Seal in jars.

Corn Relish

- 5 pints sweet corn, cut from cob
- 3 green sweet peppers
- 2 red sweet peppers
- 4 pints vinegar
- 4 pints finely chopped cabbage
- 1½ pounds sugar
- ¼ pound mustard
- 2 tablespoons salt

Seed and chop peppers. Mix all ingredients together, and cook until corn is soft, about twenty-five minutes. Seal air-tight in hot, clean jars.

Dixie Relish

- 1 quart chopped cabbage
- 1 pint chopped white onions
- 1 pint chopped sweet red peppers
- 1 pint chopped sweet green peppers
- 5 tablespoons salt
- 4 tablespoons mustard seed
- 2 tablespoons celery seed
- ¾ cup sugar
- 1 quart cider vinegar

Remove seeds and coarse, white sections from peppers, and put through meat grinder. Soak in brine for twenty-four hours, and drain. Chop cabbage, onions, and peppers before measuring. Combine; add spices, sugar, and vinegar. Let stand over night in covered crock. Pack in sterilized jars, adjust rubber, cover, and partly seal. Process for fifteen minutes, having water just simmering, below the boiling point.

Southern Relish

2 quarts sweet corn, uncooked	1 quart vinegar
4 pounds cabbage	4 cups sugar
1 quart butter beans	1½ cups flour
3 large onions	1 cup salt
3 green sweet peppers	½ cup dry mustard
3 red peppers (medium size)	2 teaspoons turmeric powder
	2 quarts vinegar

Measure corn after cutting from the cob. Remove seeds from peppers. Add cabbage, onions, and peppers, chopped fine. Cut beans in small pieces. Combine all vegetables; add one quart of vinegar, and boil twenty minutes. Mix dry ingredients in a separate bowl, with a little cold water, to form a smooth paste; add two quarts vinegar, boiling hot, and cook until creamy. Pour over vegetables, and cook until corn and cabbage are soft. Seal hot in jars. This will keep two years.

Tomato Relish

1 peck ripe tomatoes	2 red peppers
1 dozen sour apples	2 tablespoons salt
1 quart onions	1 pint vinegar
3 green peppers	½ teaspoon cayenne

Scald tomatoes; peel and quarter. Pare apples, core, and chop fine. Put onions and peppers through meat grinder, after removing seeds. Combine vegetables; add vinegar and salt, and cook until vegetables are soft. Seal hot.

Chili Sauce
1803

18 ripe tomatoes	1 cup brown sugar
1 large onion	2½ cups vinegar
3 green sweet peppers	2 teaspoons salt

1 teaspoon each cinnamon, allspice, clove, nutmeg

Scald and peel tomatoes. Chop onions fine. Remove seeds from peppers, and chop fine. Combine vegetables, add other ingredients, and cook until mixture thickens. Seal in bottles when cold.

India Chowchow

½ peck ripe tomatoes	3 small red peppers
¼ peck green tomatoes	3 quarts white button onions
1 quart large green cucumbers	1 head cauliflower

1 bunch celery

Peel and slice cucumbers. Break cauliflower into flowerets, and chop green tomatoes. Cut celery in small pieces, peel onions, and remove seeds from peppers. Chop peppers fine. Combine these six vegetables, and put to soak in brine for twenty-four hours. Cook for twenty minutes, and drain thoroughly. Make a mustard sauce as follows:

2 quarts vinegar	1 tablespoon celery seed
6 tablespoons mustard	1 tablespoon mustard seed
1 tablespoon turmeric powder	1 teaspoon curry powder
1 cup flour	2 cups sugar

Mix dry ingredients in a large bowl, with a little cold water, to form a smooth paste. Add vinegar, boiling hot, and cook until creamy. Peel ripe tomatoes and add to drained vegetables. Pour mustard sauce over all vegetables, and cook until tomatoes are soft. Bottle hot.

Piccalilli

1 peck green tomatoes	½ teaspoon cayenne
8 large onions	2 tablespoons black pepper
2 red peppers	½ pound white mustard seed
1 cup salt	¼ pound celery seed
1½ pounds white sugar	1 ounce whole clove
1 quart vinegar	2 tablespoons allspice

Chop tomatoes fine and slice onions thin. Remove seeds from peppers and put through meat grinder. Combine all vegetables; add salt, and let stand over night. In the morning, drain well. Add other ingredients (clove and allspice tied in a muslin bag), and cook until vegetables are soft. Remove spice bag and seal hot.

MISCELLANEOUS CONTRIBUTED RECIPES

WHILE there is such need of sugar, recipes calling for a large amount should either be made in small amounts and used in place of butter, or their use should be postponed till more normal conditions are restored.

To be sure that preserves, butters, jams, and marmalades will keep indefinitely, it is necessary to process them after filling and partially sealing the jars. Place the filled jars in hot water bath; have the water come well over the jars and process ten minutes, keeping the water just at the boiling point. Be as careful in sealing preserves, butters, etc., as in sealing fruits and vegetables. Always use a new rubber.

Quince Honey

6 quinces 3 cups water 3 pounds sugar

Pare quinces; quarter, core, put through meat grinder, and cover with cold water. Cook ten minutes. Add sugar, and cook three-quarters of an hour. Seal hot in jars.

Pear Honey

May be made the same as quince honey, using hard variety of pears.

Cherry Preserve

12 quarts cherries 3 pounds sugar
3 quarts red currants 10 whole cloves
$\frac{1}{2}$ ounce stick cinnamon

Remove stones from cherries. Put currants in preserving kettle; crush, and bring to the boil. Drain in cheesecloth bag. To the cherries add sugar, currant juice, and spices tied in a bag, and boil twenty minutes or longer, depending on the amount of water in the currants used. The mixture, when cooked, should be the consistency of marmalade. Seal in one-half pint jars.

Preserved Figs

3 pounds dried figs 4 lemons
3 pounds granulated sugar 1 ounce green ginger

Buy the finest whole figs; separate, and wipe each fig with a damp cloth. Soak the figs over night in cold water to cover. Drain; add fresh water to cover figs, and simmer slowly until they are soft. Lift each one out carefully, without breaking, and set to cool. Add sugar to the water in which the figs were cooked, and cook until medium thick syrup is obtained. Put the figs back into the syrup; add the juice of the lemons, the rind of two, and the bits of green ginger. Simmer all together for ten minutes. Remove the figs, and set them to dry slightly in the oven. Boil the syrup down until thick. Put the figs in glass jars, pour syrup over them, and seal while hot.

Preserved Peaches

Blanch nine pounds of clingstone peaches in boiling water two minutes; dip in cold water and slip off the skins. To seven pounds of white sugar add one and one-half quarts of hot water, and dissolve over the fire. Bring to the boiling point and add the peaches, a few at a time. When tender, pack in hot jars. If the syrup is thin, after the peaches are cooked in it, boil down until thick. Pour over peaches, and seal.

Those who wish their peaches brandied will add equal parts of white brandy to syrup.

Citron Melon Preserve

| Citron melon | Lemons |
| Sugar | Preserved ginger |

Cut the melon in quarters. Peel, and cut up into inch cubes. Cover with boiling water and cook until tender. Remove from water and drain in colander. For each pound of melon allow three-quarters pound of sugar, one lemon, and one ounce of preserved ginger. Slice the lemons thin, discarding the seeds; cut ginger in small pieces, and cook lemon and ginger in water to cover until lemons are soft. Then add sugar and water, using one-half as much water as sugar. Cook all together until syrup is thick. Add the melon, and let stand over night. In the morning, heat, and simmer slowly one-half hour. Remove melon from syrup, and put into hot jars. Boil syrup down until thick, and pour over the rind. Seal.

Watermelon Preserve

Proceed as for citron melon, above. Discard pink portion and use only the rind, after peeling. The discarded portion can be iced and used for dessert.

Spiced Currant

5 quarts currants	1 teaspoon cloves
1 pint vinegar	1 teaspoon cinnamon
3 pounds sugar	1 teaspoon allspice

Combine ingredients and cook one hour. Seal in jars.

Economical Spiced Grape

5 pounds Concord grapes	2 teaspoons cinnamon
3 pounds sugar	1 teaspoon allspice
½ pint vinegar	½ teaspoon clove

Pulp the grapes; cover the skins with water, and cook until tender. Cook the pulp separately and strain out the seeds. Combine with the skins; add sugar, spices, and vinegar. Boil slowly until the mixture thickens. Seal hot in jars, and process ten minutes.

Spiced Pears

7 pounds hard pears	2 ounces preserved ginger
4 pounds sugar	1 lemon
1 pint vinegar	2 ounces stick cinnamon
2 tablespoons whole clove	

Peel, quarter, and core the pears. Make a syrup of vinegar and sugar. Put spices in cheesecloth bag and boil in syrup for ten minutes. Add pears, lemon rind grated, and ginger cut in small pieces. Cook until pears are soft. Pack into hot jars, and boil syrup down. When thick, add to fruit in jars. Seal while hot.

Ginger Pears

8 pounds hard pears	3 lemons
6 pounds sugar	1 pound sugared ginger
¼ pound ginger root	

Peel pears and chop fine. Put sugar in preserve kettle; add one quart of water, juice of lemons, and rinds cut fine. Bring to the boiling point; add pears, sugared ginger cut fine, and ginger root chopped fine and tied in a bag. Cook slowly until pears are soft and syrup is thick.

Chilicoque

6 pounds rhubarb
5½ pounds sugar
1 pound figs
2 lemons

Cut up rhubarb; add sugar, and let stand over night. In the morning, add figs, washed, and lemons, cut in thin slices. Cook slowly three hours. Seal in jars.

Cherry Delight

3 pounds ripe cherries
1 pound dried currants
1 pound rhubarb
4 pounds sugar
1 pound walnuts
6 oranges

Stone cherries; wash, and add currants, rhubarb cut fine, sugar, juice and grated rind of oranges, and walnuts chopped fine. Cook until thick. Seal in jars.

Cranberry Conserve

Contributed by Mrs. Tent

5 cups cranberries
¾ cup cold water
4 cups sugar
1 cup raisins
½ cup English walnuts
1½ oranges
¾ cup boiling water

Combine cranberries and cold water. Cook until soft, and rub through a strainer. Chop walnuts and raisins; slice oranges thin (do not remove skin). Combine all ingredients except the nuts, and cook twenty minutes after boiling point is reached. Add nuts five minutes before removing from the fire. Seal in jars.

Fig and Rhubarb Conserve

5 pounds rhubarb   2 pounds figs
5 pounds sugar   2 lemons (juice)

Cut rhubarb in small pieces; add figs cut up, and lemon juice. Cover with sugar, and let stand over night. In the morning, boil gently for one and one-half hours.

Grape Conserve

3 pounds grapes   1 pound seeded raisins
3 pounds sugar   2 lemons
3 medium-sized oranges

Wash grapes; mash, and cook in porcelain kettle until soft. Strain through a sieve. Add sugar, raisins chopped well, and juice of two lemons. Add lemon rinds flaked in small pieces. Add oranges cut in thin slices. Cook one and one-half hours. Seal while hot.

Rhubarb and Orange Conserve

6 cups rhubarb   2 cups orange pulp
8 cups sugar

Cut rhubarb into small pieces; add orange pulp and sugar, and cook slowly one hour. A little water may be added if necessary.

Strawberry and Pineapple Conserve

2 pineapples, cut in cubes   3 quarts strawberries
  after peeling   4 pounds sugar

Boil all together until consistency of jam. Stir occasionally, to keep from burning. Seal in jars, and process for five minutes.

Green Tomato Conserve

12 pounds green tomatoes   1 ounce ginger root
8 pounds white sugar   3 sliced lemons

Slice tomatoes and drain over night. Put sugar and one pint of water in preserving kettle. When sugar is dissolved, add tomatoes, and simmer slowly four hours. Add ginger root chopped fine, and lemons sliced thin. Cook one-half hour longer. Seal in jars.

Yellow Tomato Conserve

2 quarts pear-shaped yellow tomatoes
2 lemons
1 cup seeded raisins
2½ pounds sugar
4 tablespoons thinly sliced candied ginger
½ teaspoon salt

Put the tomatoes in preserving kettle; sprinkle sugar and salt over the top, and stir and break with wooden spoon until sugar is dissolved. Add grated rind of lemon, lemon juice, ginger, and raisins chopped fine. Cook until mixture is consistency of marmalade. Seal in one-half pint jars, and process ten minutes.

Apple Butter

4 quarts apples   2 ounces ginger root
2 lemons   Sugar by weight

Pare and chop apples. Make a syrup, using one pound of sugar to each pound of fruit. Measure the amount of sugar, add equal measure of water, and boil until syrup is thick. To syrup add grated rinds and juice of lemons, ginger root chopped fine, and apples, and cook until consistency of jam. Seal air-tight in jelly glasses or pint jars. Cover with melted paraffin if jelly glasses are used.

Old-fashioned Apple Butter

Use the sound portion of windfall, wormy, or bruised apples to make into butter. The early summer varieties do not make good apple butter. Use the late, good cooking apple for this purpose. Boil sweet cider, just from the press, in a porcelain-lined kettle until reduced one-half. Pare, core, and quarter apples. Put into reduced cider, and boil until apples are tender. Put in as many apples as the cider will cover. Stir constantly, and cook until the consistency of marmalade. Just before removing from the fire, add two teaspoonfuls of ground cinnamon, half a teaspoon of clove, and one-half teaspoon of grated nutmeg to each quart of apple butter. This will keep in a stone crock, or may be stored in jars. Sugar to taste may be added, if desired, in the last quarter of cooking. No hard and fast rule applies to spices, as individual taste may be followed largely.

Blackberry, Raspberry, or Strawberry Jam

Pick over the fruit; allow three-fourths of a pound of sugar to each pound of fruit. Crush the berries in a porcelain-lined or agate kettle, and put over fire. Heat the sugar in the oven, and after berries are heated through add one-third the sugar. Boil slowly for ten minutes, and add one-half the remaining sugar. Boil ten minutes more, and add remaining sugar. Cook until thick enough to spread, and pour into glasses taken from hot water. Seal with melted paraffin when cold.

Blackberry Jam
A very old recipe

For each pint of blackberries use three-fourths pound of brown sugar. Pick over berries and mash slightly. Add sugar, and cook slowly until thick. Seal in jelly glasses.

Gooseberry Jam

6 pounds ripe gooseberries   5 pounds sugar
3 cups red currant juice

Pick over the berries; remove blossom ends, and mash with a silver fork. Add currant juice to sugar, and heat through. Add berries, and boil gently for one hour, skimming as needed. Let stand over night, and next day cook again until thick. Pour into glasses taken from hot water, and seal with melted paraffin when cold.

Amber Marmalade

1 orange   1 grapefruit
1 lemon   Sugar by measure

Cut up fruit with scissors or put through a meat chopper, rejecting nothing but seeds and core. Measure fruit, and add to it three times as much water. Let stand over night, and in the morning boil ten minutes. Let stand over night again, and the second morning add pint for pint of sugar. Boil steadily until it is thick enough to spread. Too long boiling is apt to caramelize it. This recipe will make twelve glasses.

Peach Marmalade

Second quality peaches may be used for making marmalade. Blanch in boiling water for two minutes; plunge into cold water, and slip off skins. Remove stones, and quarter. Put in a preserving kettle and add an equal weight of sugar, the juice of a lemon to every two and one-half pounds of fruit, and nutmeg to flavor slightly. Cook slowly on the back of the stove until the consistency of jam. Seal in glasses. Other spices may be substituted for nutmeg, but some spice greatly improves the flavor of the marmalade.

Mock Marmalade

3 pounds carrots   6 lemons
3 pounds sugar   2 ounces blanched almonds

Scrape carrots; boil in water until tender. Put through a meat chopper, with the almonds and thin rind of the lemons. Add sugar, juice of lemons, and cook to the consistency of marmalade.

Orange Marmalade

Contributed by Miss Louisa Sohier

1 dozen oranges   4 quarts cold water
4 lemons   8 pounds fine granulated sugar

Choose thin-skinned oranges. Wipe, and cut fruit fine, peel and all. Add cold water; let stand thirty-six hours, then boil the mixture two hours. Add sugar, and boil one and one-half hours. Seal in jelly glasses or one-half pint jars.

Apple and Barberry Spread

2 quarts stemmed barberries $1\frac{1}{2}$ quarts molasses
4 quarts apples   1 pint sugar

Wash, pick over, and stem barberries. Add sugar and molasses, and cook until soft. Add apples, peeled and quartered, and cook slowly on the back of the stove until apples are tender. Seal in jars, and process ten minutes.

Quince Spread

8 quinces   4 Baldwin apples
Sugar

Peel and core quinces. Cut in cubes; cover with boiling water, and cook until tender. Drain, saving the water. Peel and quarter apples; cook until tender in the water drained from the quinces. Drain, measure liquid, and add equal measure of sugar. Boil ten minutes. Combine quinces and apples and pour syrup over them, and simmer slowly one hour. Seal in jelly tumblers. (Delicious for children's sandwiches.)

Mincemeat

1880

- 6 pounds cooked meat (beef or tongue), chopped
- 3 pounds raisins, chopped
- 3 pounds currants
- 2 pounds citron, chopped
- 2 pounds suet, chopped
- 4 pounds brown sugar
- 2 cups sweet cider
- 2 cups liquid in which meat has boiled
- 2 tablespoons allspice
- 2 tablespoons mace
- 2 tablespoons clove
- 2 tablespoons cinnamon
- 3 tablespoons salt

Combine ingredients, and cook slowly one hour. When making pies, add apples, one part to two of mincemeat.

The original recipe called for one pint of sherry wine and one-half pint of brandy, but fruit juices may be substituted, or the wine and brandy may be omitted from the recipe without in any way spoiling results.

Mincemeat
Cheshire, England

1 pound beef
1 pound suet
¼ pound preserved lemon peel
¼ pound preserved orange peel
1 pound currants
1 pound raisins
3 quarts apples, chopped, with peel on
3 cups sugar
2 glasses currant jelly
1 cup boiled-down cider
1 tablespoon salt
1 tablespoon clove
1 tablespoon nutmeg
1 tablespoon ginger
1 tablespoon cinnamon

Cook beef, and chop fine with suet. Add other ingredients, and cook ten minutes. Seal hot in jars. Adjust rubber, cover, and partially seal. Process ten minutes in hot water bath. Mincemeat which is to be used at once will keep without processing. Simply seal air-tight.

The original recipe calls for one cup of brandy. Fruit juices may be used instead, with satisfactory result.

Vegetable Mincemeat
Newton Centre

    1 peck green tomatoes (chop and drain)
    2 lemons, chopped fine
    3 pounds brown sugar
    2 pounds white sugar

Boil the above for two and one-half hours, slowly. Then add

    ½ peck apples, chopped fine
    3 pounds raisins, chopped fine
    ½ pound blanched almonds, chopped
    1 cup boiled-down sweet cider
    1 cup vinegar
    1 glass currant jelly
    1 tablespoon vegetable oil
    2 teaspoons each cinnamon and clove
    1 teaspoon each allspice and nutmeg
    Salt to taste

Cook until apples are clear. Seal in jars hot. Process ten minutes.

DRY YOUR VEGETABLES AND FRUITS

ALONG with the work of canning and preserving goes the simple process of drying. Throughout Europe this work is extensively carried on, and in Germany, particularly, the dried product has been an important economic factor, for the German army has been to a large measure sustained on dehydrated products.

Dried fruits, such as apricots, prunes, figs, apples, dates, raisins, etc., are familiar to all, and are used in every household. Other articles of food may be dried as successfully and are just as palatable. Much wisdom in drying comes with but very little experience. As in canning, certain rules must be followed for success, else the material will sour and mold, and be unfit to serve on the table.

Drying may take the place of canning when storage facilities are limited, when jars are expensive and scarce, or when there is but little to conserve. It may supplement canning when there is a great surplus, that the entire product be conserved. Drying may also be recommended for the housewife who is in delicate health, and finds canning laborious work, since drying may be said to take care of itself, once the material is in place and a few general directions have been carried out.

An empty room or the attic makes an excellent drying place, providing there is a current of air passing through; otherwise the product will mold. Never put vegetables on the floor to dry, and do not spread them out on a table. *It is absolutely necessary that air circulate under and over the material.*

Sun Drying. Drying may be done in the sun, but except in the hottest weather it should not be attempted. Get a good exposure, where the sun will be all day on the material. The top of a flat-roofed house is an excellent drying post, and is away from the dust of the street. Sun drying is easy and cheap, but care must be taken to cover the material with mosquito netting, that flies and insects cannot attack the foods.

In all drying, be sure that there is free circulation *under* the material to be dried, as well as *over* it.

Have a wire-mesh frame set up on four posts, about three feet from the ground or roof. Cover with cheesecloth, and spread fruit or vegetables out carefully in single layers to dry. The material will not dry uniformly if carelessly spread out and allowed to overlap. If long-continued hot, dry weather is expected, it is not necessary to bring the foods in at night. Where the frame stands well above the ground, the dew does not affect the material, unless located near the sea or a river, where the dew is very heavy. Much unnecessary labor can be eliminated by leaving the material out over night.

Spread a piece of oilcloth over the top of the wire frame at night, to keep the dampness out. Do not let the oilcloth rest on the material, but fasten it in the posts at the sides. This should be removed early in the morning.

Oven Drying. Arrange the material to be dried on plates, or perforated containers, or racks, and put in the oven. The fire should be low and the oven door be left open. When small quantities are to be dried at a time, this method is the quickest and the easiest for the housewife. Six to eight hours is the time required for most products that are oven dried.

Commercial Dryers. There are commercial dryers on the market which may be set over the gas range or kitchen stove. One of the most practical is of the type of a large, flat tin box, into which water is poured through a small tunnel. The dryer, partly filled with water, is set on the range; the material is spread out on top of the dryer; the water heats gradually, and the material is soon dried.

Be sure the products are sufficiently dried before putting away, or they will mold.

Packing and Storing. Containers for storing dried products must be moisture proof. Tin cans, glass jars, heavy paper bags, and cardboard boxes make good containers. If paper bags or boxes are used, put them where rats and insects will not get at them.

Dried Vegetables

Corn. Corn is without question the most satisfactory of all vegetables to dry. Never dry it in the sun. Corn requires heat above the temperature of the sun's rays (unless the day is very hot), and unless quickly dried it sours. Well-developed, sweet ears should be chosen. Blanch in boiling water three minutes. Plunge in cold water, to set the milk. With a sharp knife cut the corn from the cob, being careful not to cut into the cob. Spread thinly on platters. Place in moderate oven or on commercial drier, and leave until it is hard and will rattle. It is necessary to turn the corn several times with a knife, during the process of drying. It will look very much like the broken corn fed to chickens.

When wanted, soak corn in cold water for four hours,

or over night. Cook in the same water until soft. Add butter or butter substitute, cream, salt, and pepper before serving.

String Beans. Never attempt to dry any but fresh, green beans, with tender pods. String the beans and cut the pods in strips lengthwise. Spread thinly on platters, or put out of doors on cheesecloth on wire rack. Leave until well shriveled up and leathery. Beans should not be brittle and snap. When they have reached this stage, they are dried too much, and will be tough when eaten. It is not necessary to turn the beans, for they will dry without further attention, once they are thinly spread out to the heat. Store in paper bags or pasteboard boxes.

To use, cover with cold water and soak over night. Cook in the same water until soft. Season to taste.

Lima Beans. Shell the beans, and spread out in the sun to dry. Sun drying usually takes three days. With a commercial drier, they dry in from three to six hours.

Celery or Mint Leaves. Wash and spread leaves on a platter, and put in the oven. When thoroughly dry, crush the leaves with a rolling pin, put in bottles, label, and use for flavoring.

Egg Plant. Egg plant should be dried by artificial heat, either in the oven or on a commercial drier. If dried in the sun, which is a longer process, it will turn dark.

Peel the egg plant, cut in slices one-half inch thick, and cut the slices up into cubes. Place in the oven on plates, or put on a drier, and leave until the egg plant is dry and leathery.

To use, soak over night and prepare as fresh egg plant.

Onions, Carrots, Turnips. When winter vegetables can be kept in root cellars, it is better not to dry them. For those who live in apartments, however, it is convenient to dry these vegetables, and to have them on hand for soups. Slice onions thin, and dry in the oven. Carrots and turnips also dry quickly in the oven. They should first be scraped and then sliced thin.

In making a vegetable or meat soup, flavor with dried vegetables. No preparation is necessary. Simply add a half-cupful of dried carrots, turnips, onions, or whatever is desired.

Peas. Peas, like corn, require quick drying, or they will mold. Do not blanch. Shell; spread out thinly, either out of doors on a wire frame or on platters in the oven. When dry, peas look shriveled and are hard.

To prepare for the table, soak in cold water until they have taken on their regular size and appearance. Cook in the same water until soft, and add butter or butter substitute and seasoning.

Peppers. Split sweet peppers and remove seeds. If the weather is hot, begin drying out of doors and finish in the oven.

To prepare for the table, soak in water four hours, or until the peppers have taken up moisture enough to be of good size. Stuff, or cut up, and use as flavoring in hash or soup.

Spinach, Beet Tops, or Parsley. Wash. Pick leaves from stems and spread out to dry, either out of doors in the sun or in the oven. Two to three days is necessary for drying spinach out of doors. With a commercial drier, this can be accomplished in six hours.

Italian Tomato Paste

1 bushel tomatoes	1 carrot, chopped fine
2 large onions, chopped fine	1 bunch parsley

Wash tomatoes (they should be very ripe), remove stems; break into a kettle, skins and all. Add onions, carrot, and parsley. Boil slowly five hours. Pour into a cheesecloth bag of two thicknesses, and drain thoroughly without squeezing the bag. Press contents of bag through a fine sieve, until nothing is left but skins and seeds. Add salt to taste, and put out of doors in hot sun on platters, under glass if possible. Take in at night, and if uncovered protect from insects with a piece of cheesecloth. Paste is ready when it can be rolled in a ball and is the consistency of butter. Put in sterilized jar, with bits of bay leaf. Fill jar to one-half inch of top, and cover with olive oil. This makes a good seal. Replace oil after using paste. Use paste for flavoring soups, meat dishes, etc.

Dried Fruits

Apples. It is not advisable to dry early varieties of apples, since they lack firmness and flavor. Peel, core, and slice apples in rings one-fourth inch in thickness. Arrange slices in rows on trays. Place in the sun or dry in the oven. Sun drying usually requires three or four days, while drying in the oven or with the commercial drier is very much quicker. The texture of the dried apple should be leathery, velvety, and soft.

Peaches. Cut in halves and remove stones. Dry without removing the skin. Place on commercial drier, or on platters in the oven, with pit side up. Sprinkle lightly with sugar, and leave until shriveled and leathery. When dried, the peaches will look much like dried apricots.

Pears. Pare, core, and cut fruit in eighths. Use sun drying or commercial evaporator, depending on weather conditions. Pears should be dried quickly, or they will discolor. **Quinces** may be dried in the same way.

Blueberries and Huckleberries. Spread on trays and dry in the oven, or out of doors if the day is hot. Most excellent used in berry cakes or pies.

Raspberries. Dry in the sun if the day is hot, or spread on plates and dry in the oven. If a commercial drier is used, the surface of the drier must not be allowed to get too hot, or the berries will cook. Raspberries will dry in the oven in about three hours. The temperature of the oven should be increased from 125° F. to 140° F. during the period of drying. Too hot an oven will tend to cook the berries.

INDEX

Alcohol Test for Pectin, 42, 43
Amber Marmalade, 80
Apple Butter, 78, 79
    Jelly, 45
        from Parings, 46
        Spiced, 46
        Variations, 46
    Juice, 51
    Sauce, 34
Apple and Barberry Spread, 81
Apples, 34
    Dried, 90
Asparagus, 17

Bacteria, 4
Bag, Jelly, 44
Barberry Jelly, 47
    Spread, Apple and, 81
Beans, Baked, 18
    Lima, 18
        Dried, 88
    Shell, 18
    String, 17
        Dried, 88
        Pickled, 56
Beef Stew, 31
Beet Tops, Dried, 89
Beets, 12, 19
    Pickled, 57
Berries, Time Table for, 39
Blackberry Jam, 79, 80
    Juice, 51
Blackberries, 36
Blanching, 1
Blueberry Jelly, 47
Blueberries, 36
    Dried, 91

Bordeaux Relish, 67
Bottling Fruit Juices, 52
Botulism, 15
Brine, 56
Bubbles, 11

Canner, Steam Pressure, 5
Canning, Cost of, 14
    Fractional Method, 5
    Intermittent Method, 5
    Preparation for, 1
Cans, Tin, 13
Cape Cod Pepper Relish, 67
Carrots, 19
    Dried, 89
Cauliflower, 20
Celery Leaves, Dried, 88
    Pickle, 58
Cherry Delight, 76
    Juice, 51
    Preserve, 72
Cherries, Sour, 36
    Sweet, 36
        Pickled, 61
Chicken, 30
Chilicoque, 76
Chili Sauce, 70
Chinese Cabbage Leaves, 21
Chowchow, India, 70
Chowder, 31
Chuddy, Peach, 66
Chutney, Sweet Indian, 66
Citron Melon Preserve, 74
Cold Water Method for Preserving Fruit, 40
Conserve, Cranberry, 76
    Fig and Rhubarb, 77

INDEX

Conserve, Grape, 77
   Rhubarb and Orange, 77
   Strawberry and Pineapple, 77
   Green Tomato, 78
   Yellow Tomato, 78
Corn, Canned, 20
   Dried, 87
   Pickled, 57
   Relish, 68
Cost of Canning, 14
Cover Jelly, To, 45
Crabapple Jelly, 47
Crabapples, Sweet Pickled, 62
Cranberry Conserve, 76
   Jelly, 47
   Ketchup, 64
Cranberries, 36, 40
Cucumber Pickle, Ripe, 62
   Uncooked, 59
Cucumbers, Canned, 58
   Pickled, 58
Currant Jelly, 48
   Juice, 51
   Spiced, 74
Currants, 36

Dandelion Greens, 21
   Shrub, 54
Dixie Relish, 68
Dryers, Commercial, 87
Drying Fruits and Vegetables, 85
Duck, 30
Dutch Salad, 61

Egg Plant, Canned, 21
   Dried, 88
Elderberry Jelly, 48
Equipment, 7
Extraction, Second, 43

Failures, 6
   in Jelly Making, 42
Fig and Rhubarb Conserve, 77

Figs, Preserved, 73
Fish, 31
Flat-sour, 12
Fractional Method of Canning, 5
Fricassees, 31
Fruit Juices, 51
   Bottling, 52
   Processing, 52
   Sealing, 53
Fruit Juices, Apple, 51
   Blackberry, 51
   Cherry, 51
   Currant, 51
   Grape, 51, 54
   Raspberry, 51
   Strawberry, 51, 53
Fruit, Sun-cooked, 37
   Cold Water Method for Preserving, 40
   Time Table for, 39

Game, 30
Ginger Pears, 75
Gooseberry Jam, 80
   Ketchup, 64
Gooseberries, 36, 40
Governor Sauce, 65
Grape Conserve, 77
   Economical Spiced, 75
   Jelly, 48
      Green, 49
   Juice, 51, 54
      Sherbet, 55
   Ketchup, 64
   Tapioca, 55
Green Tomato Pickle, 60
Greens, 21

Halibut, 31
Honey, 44
   Pear, 72
   Quince, 72
Huckleberries, 36
   Dried, 91

India Chowchow, 70
Indian Chutney, Sweet, 66
Intermittent Method of Canning, 5
Irish Stew, 31
Italian Tomato Paste, 90

Jam, Blackberry, 79, 80
　Gooseberry, 80
　Raspberry, 79
　Strawberry, 79
Jars, 7, 10, 11, 13
　To Open, 15
　Cheap, 7
Jelly Bag, 44
Jelly, To Cover, 45
　Making, 41
　　Failures in, 42
　　General Rules for, 42
Jelly, Apple, 45
　from Parings, 46
　Spiced, 46
　Barberry, 47
　Blueberry, 47
　Crabapple, 47
　Cranberry, 47
　Currant, 48
　Elderberry, 48
　Grape, 48
　　Green, 49
　Mint, 49
　Quince, 49
　Raspberry, 49
　Strawberry, 50
　Triple Fruit, 50
Juices, Fruit, 51, 52, 53
Julienne Soup Mixture, 28

Kale, 21
Ketchup, Cranberry, 64
　Gooseberry, 64
　Grape, 64
　Tomato, 65

Lamb Stew, 31
Left-overs, Meat, 31
Light, Protection from, 13
Lima Beans, 18
　Dried, 88
Loganberries, 36

Mackerel, 31
Marlborough Pickle, Sweet, 62
Marmalade, Amber, 80
　Mock, 81
　Orange, 81
　Peach, 80
Meat, 30
　Left-overs, 31
Microörganisms, 4
Mincemeat, 82, 83
　Vegetable, 84
Mint Jelly, 49
　Leaves, Dried, 88
Mock Marmalade, 81
Molds, 4, 13
Mustard Pickle, 59

Necessity for Following Time Tables, 6

Okra, Corn, and Tomato Soup Mixture, 28
Onions, Dried, 89
Orange Conserve, Rhubarb and, 77
　Marmalade, 81
Oven Drying, 86

Packing, 2
Paraffin, 45
Parsley, Dried, 89
Peach Chuddy, 66
　Marmalade, 80
　Pickle, Sweet, 63
Peaches, 34
　Dried, 90
　Preserved, 73

INDEX

Pear Honey, 72
Pears, 35
  Dried, 91
  Ginger, 75
  Spiced, 75
Peas, 22
  Dried, 89
Pectin, 41
  Alcohol Test for, 42, 43
Peppers, 23
  Dried, 89
Philadelphia Pickle, 60
Piccalilli, 71
Pickle, Celery, 58
  Chopped, 59
  Cucumber, Ripe, 62
    Uncooked, 59
  Green Tomato, 60
  Mustard, 59
  Philadelphia, 60
  Sweet Marlborough, 62
  Sweet Peach, 63
Pickled String Beans, 56
  Beets, 57
  Cherries, Sweet, 61
  Corn, 57
  Crabapples, Sweet, 62
  Cucumbers, 58
  Watermelon Rind, 63
Pickling, 56
Pineapple, 35
  Conserve, Strawberry and, 77
Plums, 35
Plunging, 2
Preparation for Canning, 1
  of Home-Canned Products for the Table, 15
Preserve, Cherry, 72
  Citron Melon, 74
  Watermelon, 74
Preserved Figs, 73
  Peaches, 73
Preserving Powders, 13

Processing, 3
  Correct, 4

Quince Honey, 72
  Jelly, 49
  Spread, 82
Quinces, Dried, 91

Rack in Boiler, 3, 11, 52
Raspberry Jam, 79
  Jelly, 49
  Juice, 51
  Tapioca, 55
  Vinegar, 54
Raspberries, 36, 38
  Dried, 91
Relish, Bordeaux, 67
  Cape Cod Pepper, 67
  Corn, 68
  Dixie, 68
  Southern, 69
  Tomato, 69
Rhubarb, 35, 40
  Conserve, Fig and, 77
  and Orange Conserve, 77
Rubber Rings, 8, 10, 13

Salmon, 31
Sauce, Chili, 70
  Governor, 65
Second Extraction, 43
Seal, Testing the, 4
Sealing, 3
  Fruit Juices, 53
Shell Beans, 18
Shrinkage, 12
Sherbet, Grape, 55
Soup Mixtures, 27
  Tomato, 28
Southern Relish, 69
Spiced Apple Jelly, 46
  Currant, 74
  Grape, 75
  Pears, 75

Spinach, 21
　Dried, 89
Steam Pressure Canner, 5
Sterilizers, 8
Stew, Beef, 31
　Irish, 31
　Lamb, 31
Storage, 12, 87
Strawberry Jam, 79
　Jelly, 50
　Juice, 51, 53
　and Pineapple Conserve, 77
Strawberries, 36, 37
　Sun-cooked, 37
String Beans, 17
　Dried, 88
　Pickled, 56
Succotash, 23
Summer Squash, 24
Sun-cooked Fruit, 37
Sun Drying, 86
Swiss Chard, 21
Syrups, 32

Tapioca, Grape, 55
　Raspberry, 55
Test, Alcohol, 42, 43
　Two-Drop, 44
Testing the Seal, 4
Time Table for Fruit and Berries, 39
　for Vegetables, 26
Time Tables, 6

Tin Cans, 13
Tomato, Bean, and Okra Soup Mixture, 28
　Conserve, Green, 78
　　Yellow, 78
　Cream, 67
　Ketchup, 65
　Paste, Italian, 90
　Pickle, Green, 60
　Purée, 29
　Relish, 69
　Soup, 28
Tomatoes, 24
Triple Fruit Jelly, 50
Trout, 31
Turkey, 30
Turnips, Dried, 89
Two-Drop Test, 44

Utensils, 9

Vegetable Mincemeat, 84
Vegetables, 17
　Time Table for, 26

Water Method for Preserving Fruit, Cold, 40
　in Processing, 3, 11
Watermelon Rind, Pickled, 63
　Preserve, 74
Winter Vegetables, 25

Yeasts, 4

LCD

WITHDRAWN FROM
BUFFALO
&
ERIE COUNTY
PUBLIC LIBRARY